CRYSTAL WITCHCRAFT FOR BEGINNERS

A 5-STEP GUIDE TO CAST SPELLS, HARNESS THE
POWER OF HEALING STONES AND CRYSTALS FOR
WITCHES TO UNLOCK THE MIND, CHAKRAS, ENERGY
PROTECTION, AND EMOTIONAL HEALING

ESTELLE A. HARPER

Free Gifts For Our Readers!

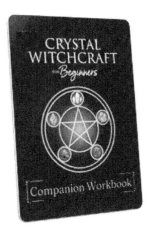

Get Free access to:

- The Crystal Witchcraft for Beginners: **Companion Workbook**
- 7 Day Guide to Perform Your Own Crystal Spell
- **All our future books**

Or Scan The QR Code

CONTENTS

WELCOME TO THE WORLD OF CRYSTALS

Witchcraft is a beautiful, spiritual practice that allows us to connect with the Earth and the cosmos in so many ways. Through our connections with natural substances, such as gemstones and crystals, we can tap into profound energies that can heal and protect us from unwanted influences. Each crystal is unique in how it offers metaphysical healing to our bodies, minds, and souls. We came from the same Earth that these crystals come from and the same cosmos from which the Earth was created. Gemstones have so many fascinating properties that can transform our lives in ways we've only imagined.

My name is Estelle A. Harper, and throughout my life, I have always been fascinated with the powers of the natural world. Not only are crystals beautifully captivating, they also represent emotions, aspirations, and power. After going through and continuing with my spiritual awakening, I've learned how vital gemstones and crystals can be to our overall well-being. My goal is to share this knowledge as we work together to brighten your life and heal you from within.

Throughout my experiences, I've been able to learn more about spiritual healing and how to connect with the gemstones that this wonderful Earth has provided us. There is a universal connection between our bodies, the Earth, and the cosmos. This connection holds power and can heal everything from anxiety and depression to common illnesses. I've always known that this power was available, and through my studies, I've been able to awaken this universal energy from within myself. This was the start of my journey, and I hope it's the start of yours too.

When we learn to identify and awaken our internal power, there is truly nothing a witch cannot do. This power comes from believing in herself wholeheartedly while learning about the metaphysical in both her own way and the way it is presented to us in this world. A witch becomes more potent and more magical with knowledge, self-belief, and experience. This is the true power of the universal energy that I have learned to harness within myself and through the use of healing crystals and gemstones.

Because of my passion for wanting to help others, I created this book to help other people learn to become the amazing souls that nature has intended. By providing my own knowledge and by teaching others how to use them properly, I hope to touch many lives so that you too, can experience the wonderful energy that these crystals have to offer. This is the greatest gift to me as a healer, and a witch, simply knowing that I can share my gift and make a true impact on the lives of people who have been hurting for too long.

Everyone experiences stress on a daily basis. These stresses can amount to anxiety, and we may also experience depression when left untreated. These troubles can stifle us right in our steps and prevent us from living our life to the fullest. Regardless of who you are, you deserve to live a bright and happy life, free of the pain and suffering that comes from our modern, fast-paced lifestyles. Crystals can do so many beautiful things, such as absorbing negativity from our most anxious moments so that we can breathe freely and focus on more important things.

The healing power of crystals doesn't stop there. We can harness the high vibrations of certain crystals to help us heal from ailments like joint pain and allergies. There truly is a crystal for almost anything you can think of, and each one has an endless supply of power because of the intricate way that it was formed and designed by our mother Earth. And even if you are currently seeing a licensed physician for an ailment that seems beyond holistic healing, know that you can include crystals in your medical plan to amplify your health. Additionally, using crystals to remove stress and anxiety, especially when dealing with heavy burdens, allows your body to heal because negative energies no longer weigh it down.

Crystals empower us to become the people we want to be. No longer are we held down by circumstance; we have the freedom to create the lives we want to live. This empowerment is connected to the energy of the Earth and the cosmos and filters into each crystal and gemstone available. We can harness their power in the palm of our hands and forge our own path in this world.

In this book, I will walk with you as we discover the many diverse and breathtaking gemstones the Earth has to offer. We'll discuss how each one can heal in its own way and how you can tap into that energy. Learning how to identify and use gemstones properly will teach you just how important and prevalent this universal energy is and how best to use it. When we're finished, you will know how this energy feels and how it works to alleviate so many troubles that we face every day.

Come with me as we discover this incredible power that is hidden deep within and around you. Your brighter and healthier future awaits!

1

WITCHCRAFT: THE PAST, PRESENT, AND FUTURE

Witchcraft is a spiritual practice that has been a part of humanity since the dawn of time. As creatures of the Earth, we're all connected to the natural forces that govern the cosmos and the universe. This is what we consider energy, and it is this energy that we use through crystal work to heal and transcend.

With witchcraft, we learn to identify and feel the subtle energies throughout the natural world, and then we understand what they mean for each one of us. These energies can be positive or negative and can attach to objects and places alike. Throughout history, witches have learned this truth, among others, and it is their practices and work that we now reflect upon and learn from in the modern age.

WITCHCRAFT IS A SISTERHOOD

It's a brotherhood too. As witches, we unite together to create one big family of practitioners, all bound together by energy. Just like the crystals we will learn about in this book, each of us has aged through the crust of the Earth and forged into who we are today. We are connected to our ancestors by blood and flesh, holding on to our ancient past, the one that makes us magical.

To become a witch is to embrace this energy and understand that you have the power within you to make great things happen in your life and in the lives of those you care about most. You were born with this pure energy in your soul, and once you learn to feel it for yourself, you can use it in whatever way you see fit. This includes manipulating energy with crystals for healing and other purposes.

Becoming empowered as a practitioner of magic is to identify and embrace your true self. You have the power to bring happiness into your life, increase your wealth and enhance your career, and nurture love and romance. You hold the key to new opportunities, even if it feels as though all the doors are closed. The first step is to acknowledge who you truly are and to accept that this universal energy that has the power to transform your life is hiding right inside of you.

Some witches are born into families who already practice and believe in the metaphysical world. Others may find their path in time by searching out answers to their many questions about the natural world. Still, some witches take on a magical lifestyle because it comes to them before they have a chance to truly understand it. No matter how magic has come to you or how you have sought it out, the simple fact that you are interested and open to the metaphysical world shows that you are awakening to your internal power.

These powers can offer you fulfillment in knowing that you can create positive change in your world. Some witches choose to connect with a coven and practice their magic amongst others in a group setting; others like to practice alone and grow in their spiritual journey in private. Again, it doesn't matter which path you choose, only that you are comfortable with who you are and ready to look deep within to find that inner, ancient energy source that is so rightfully yours.

WHAT EXACTLY IS A WITCH?

In her simplest form, a witch is a person who is aware of their psychic abilities and believes in themselves enough to know that they have the power to create change. Think of it this way: "everything that ever is or will be" always has been. All of the material in the cosmos was created and now exists in our universe. There isn't new material, and the old material doesn't go away. It simply gets recycled and reused, just as nature does here on Earth. This means that the energy you need to rid yourself of anxiety is already there in the world around you. A witch knows how to feel for this energy by using her intuition and her empathy, and she can pull that energy from the source to manipulate it into a manifestation of her choosing.

Energy work is at the heart of magic, but many aspects of a witch are strictly about her psychic abilities. Being a psychic does not simply mean that you can foresee the future; it is a way to connect deeper with those around you. This includes people, places, and things. Sometimes witches can pick up on subtle energies on personal items from someone who has passed on. Sometimes witches can walk into a building and pick up on energies that way too. This part of being psychic is fascinating and breathtaking at times, but it can also be a little scary when it happens all of a sudden. This is another great reason why crystals are amazing at energy work and why they are such a unique addition to a witch's toolkit.

Some gemstones, such as black tourmaline, are known to absorb negative energy and abolish it. Such a crystal would be perfect for a psychic witch who likes to investigate places that are known to be haunted. Protecting herself from residual energies is just one of the many aspects of crystals and energy work.

When we speak about psychic abilities, we often mean the clairs. The first five clairs represent each of the common senses. Let's briefly look at these to better understand what it means to be psychic and why it has little to do with fortune-telling.

Clairvoyance is when a person can see visions of things that have happened or may happen or visions that involve the spirit realm. Clairvoyant psychics are often able to see apparitions quite easily.

Clairsentience is the ability to feel things that are seemingly from a metaphysical presence. This might involve a slight bit of pressure on someone's arm or the sensation that something has brushed up against your body even when nothing is there.

Clairaudience is the ability to hear things, either from within or from an external source. However, the sounds are not from any recognizable person or tangible thing in the present world. It is believed that clairaudient people receive auditory messages from the spirit realm.

Clairalience is the ability to smell what seems to be coming from the environment yet lacks an identifiable source. People who are clairalient can often smell a beloved relative who has passed on.

Clairgustance is the ability to taste what does not originate from a physical source. People who are clairgustant may taste something when reflecting on a memory. Everything about the taste, including distinct flavors and specific seasonings, will come to mind as though the person is tasting that item in the present.

Claircognizance is often considered the sixth sense, which is the ability to understand and know things without having prior knowledge. It's that intuition you feel when speaking to someone, and you just know you'll be friends. Or when you're asking someone something, and the answer comes to you before the person can explain.

With these different psychic abilities, a person easily connects to the subtle energies in the world around them. When someone tells you that they are psychic, it may mean that they have any one of these abilities, or they might even have a combination of a couple. It

CRYSTAL WITCHCRAFT FOR BEGINNERS | 21

would be rare to find someone who has mastered all six, but the ability to awaken these powers lies within all of us. Everyone has their strong suit, and we all have our weaknesses as well. Where someone is keen to understand the unknown and would thus be claircognizant, tasting things from beyond the veil might be just out of reach.

WHAT CAN A WITCH DO?

Once a witch is aware of the energy within and surrounding her, she is capable of manipulating that energy in unlimited ways. Through her practice of witchcraft, she may decide to heal others or practice privately and not reveal her power to anyone. Either way, this harkens back to ancient times when witches performed mysterious acts that were often interpreted as dangerous or even devilish to outsiders. Their powers were able to not only help others but to bring them harm. This is still true for the modern witch. She can bring both great wonder and great pain.

As a witch, one can feel things through different layers of reality and tap into different frequencies. With their mind and body aligned, witches are capable of not only knowing that the energy is present but also knowing how to harness it and control it. This is what makes a witch incredibly powerful. And once she is aware of the gifts of her ancestors and the natural world around her, nothing can hold her back.

A witch has these powers because she is drawn to nature and can feel its vibrations from her fingertips to her core. She is in harmony with the seasons and with the cycle of life as it unfolds around her. Everything from blossoming plants to decaying insects awakens her intuition.

The elements, earth, air, fire, and water, play a prominent role in a witch's practice. This is because the elements are primal and have always been a part of the universe from which we come. Of course, it took a while before water appeared, but the atoms that created water have always been there. These four elements are connected to different aspects of nature, and this connection is what we consider a correspondent. For example, the correspondence for the earth element includes the north cardinal direction and the colors green and brown. New witches can learn these truths, but once a witch connects with her intuitive energy, she will understand the correspondences without needing to be told. This is how nature works. Things, such as certain animals and specific colors, go together in harmony without question.

Witches are also deeply connected to the sun and the moon. In the same way that the Earth goes through cycles, so does the moon. Often, witches will observe the moon as a goddess that connects with emotional energy and the element of water. The moon goes through phases that directly impact the Earth itself. Pushing and pulling at the oceans, the moon sways the tides as she revolves around the Earth in perfect rhythm. This energy is not simply physical; it can be felt deep within us and used to create fantastic things such as spells and rituals.

Because witches are connected to this ancient and universal energy, they are capable of utilizing different tools to practice their magic. One way to communicate with energy is to practice divination. This typically involves reading tarot cards or an oracle deck, while some witches enjoy using runes. Whatever a witch chooses to use is up to her, but the more connected she is to herself and the energy she harnesses, the truer her intuition will be.

THE HISTORY OF WITCHCRAFT

Even though witches often work for good, aiming to help people they care most about to be healthy and succeed, some witches perform magic for negative reasons. This holds true today as it did thousands of years ago. And during a time when religion, most notably Christianity, took hold of the growing world, anything that opposed society's monotheistic views was seen as demonic.

It is strange that early practitioners of magic were seen as devil-worshippers, and this is because the devil is not a construct of a pagan faith at all. Paganism, a broad term that represents all nature-based spiritualities, is focused on the natural world. That isn't to say that pagans, like witches of both Wicca and traditional witchcraft, do not believe in demons or dangerous entities; it is just odd to say that a witch is performing the devil's work. Some witches are known to dabble in the dark arts, but the history that witchcraft has endured is definitely not one of justification by those who sought to rid the world of devil worship.

As unfortunate as the events were during the Middle Ages on through to colonial America concerning witchcraft, we have to appreciate the sacrifices that the women of that time made so that we can carry on the ancient practice of magic today. If history has taught us anything, we should not persecute and judge others for how they choose to use the natural world to their benefit, especially if their methods are pure of heart and aimed at doing good. This was the case with many misunderstood women throughout the history of witchcraft.

THE SALEM WITCH TRIALS

The Salem Witch Trials have become an infamous part of the witchcraft community. In the late 1600s, the colonial United States was a devoutly religious community that saw witchcraft as the work of the devil.[1] Thanks to two German Dominicans leading up to the Salem witch trials, a publication called "Malleus Maleficarum," which translates to "The Hammer of Witches," helped the medieval world identify, capture, and interrogate those who were believed to partake in witchcraft. This sparked controversy as the notion of dangerous witchcraft spread like wildfire throughout the world.

While paganism and other ancient beliefs that now make up the core rituals and doctrines of witchcraft and Wicca do include some demons and evil spirits, believing that a witch solely works for the devil is not a true aspect of witchcraft. It is important, though, that you understand what witchcraft means and stands for in its entirety and that you can discern the difference between one form of worship and another. This is true for all religions and spiritualities, allowing you to discover who you are and find the right path for yourself throughout your life.

The idea behind devil-based worship, specifically targeting witches in colonial New England, began as early as the 14th century in Europe. During this time, religion played a heavy role in the daily lives of European citizens and thus also impacted the new world. Because life was difficult and surviving was a struggle for these early settlers, their faith gave them hope while the fear of unfortunate events plagued them.

In Salem, Massachusetts, during the colonial era of the late 1600s, residents were fearful not only of the unknown but also of the neighboring Native American tribes and their nature-based spirituality. During these difficult times, the people of Salem were not only afraid of what they couldn't explain but also of what the people they did not understand were capable of.

In 1692, two young girls from Salem Village in Massachusetts began displaying erratic behavior, including contortions and outbursts of screaming. Due to the limitations of science at the time and people's belief that God was behind everything good and pure, a local doctor diagnosed the girls with bewitchment. Not long after, other young girls began showing the same symptoms and were later diagnosed with the same bewitch-ment. A month later, warrants were issued for the arrest of certain women within the village, thus begin-ning the Salem Witch Trials.

The Salem Witch Trials took place in May of 1692, and by June 2, they passed their first verdict. Eight days later, a woman was hanged for being a witch on what became known as Gallows Hill. Following this, several other women were hanged throughout the summer and fall of the same year. As word spread throughout the puritan population of New England, other women who were seen as witches were accused and tried in court. Some women, hoping to save themselves, confessed to their crimes as they named other women, thus increasing the number of trials and accusations.

The use of spectral evidence, which is testimony that involves visions or dreams, was a highly debated subject. Opponents of spectral evidence claimed that the proposed witches should be treated as any other criminal, such that hard evidence was necessary to condemn these women for their crimes. After the resi-dents of Massachusetts began to move past the witch trials, the governor dissolved the court and disregarded spectral evidence as proof for justification.

A bit over a year after the trials began, the governor pardoned the women who were still imprisoned.

Without the help of spectral evidence, there was no reason to condemn potentially innocent women by accusation alone.

It is widely understood that the bewitchment that afflicted the residents of Salem during this time may have been the result of a toxic fungus found in cereal grains. This fungus can cause muscle spasms and delusions, both of which were attributed to the work of witches during the late 1600s. This displays a classic example of how science can often explain things that people perceive as magic. The truth is that magic is often science that has not yet been understood.

Though the early churches aimed to rid the planet of witches, the Salem trials may have done the opposite of what was intended. After seeing the tragedy that unfolded upon the residents of Salem, people throughout colonial New England were left with more questions than answers. The use of spectral evidence is no longer valid, and one person's claims against another are no longer merited.

In the years after the Salem Witch Trials, descendants of both Pagan and witchcraft practitioners, as well as people interested in witchcraft, began embracing their beliefs in support of the memory of those who were wrongly accused. Witchcraft continued to be practiced, alongside other nature-based religions, as the world entered the Enlightenment era. But this time, people were questioning their place in the universe as concepts such as psychology began to draw attention.

Between the 18th and 20th centuries, humankind experienced many new changes to society, religion, and the study of the mind. Science continued to advance as doctors could explain things that they once attributed to the devil, thus allowing witches to embrace their nature ever more so. With all the changes that came during the 20th century, especially in the free nations where citizens had the right to choose what they believed in and how to practice those beliefs, witchcraft finally found a home in popular culture.

THE MODERN ERA OF WITCHCRAFT

Despite their efforts during the 1600s, Protestants of colonial America did not remove the traditions and histories of ancient witchcraft. Instead, some traditions gained ground, which still have traction to this day. One such tradition is the observance of Halloween. This is the day when it is believed that the veil between the physical and spiritual worlds is at its thinnest, allowing the living to communicate with the dead. Halloween is the modern term for Samhain, the witch's new year. This is when the wheel of the year begins anew, and the cycles continue on, just as they always have been for thousands of years.

In addition, legends live on, like with the riding of brooms. The term broom is believed to originate from specific plants in the ancient world. Because of its connection to nature, the hearth, and the home, brooms were soon seen as a symbol of domesticity and feminine energy.[2] In time, alongside the growing suspicion of witchcraft during the Middle Ages, accusers would announce that they saw a potential witch riding her broom through the night. Despite this, the first person to ever admit to riding a broom was a man. Guillaume Edelin confessed while under torture after being arrested in 1453. From there, witches were depicted as menacing creatures who could create toxic concoctions that would allow them to levitate. The broom is still a symbol of feminine nature, and all sorts of witches proudly own decorative ones today.

THE UNIQUE TYPES OF WITCHES

Throughout all of this, the practice of magic in witch-craft has prevailed. It is another testament to the power of nature and the strength and fortitude of our ancestors. In our modern world, spiritual practices are sometimes taboo but are often welcomed with curiosity. This has allowed many unique forms of witchcraft to emerge in their rights. Witches have forged their own pathways to finding happiness in their lives, and through those paths, we have discovered distinctive ways of practice that are truly like nothing that has ever come before.

Kitchen witches focus their energy work on their homes and gardens. They use their knowledge of cooking to create recipes that can heal and promote certain outcomes in their daily lives. Kitchen witches will often use the things found throughout their homes to create spells.

Green witches are known to be one with nature as they connect with their gardens and the plants around them. Green witches enjoy creating spells and concoctions to help heal others with simple yet sacred herbs and flowers.

A hedge witch is known to "jump the hedge." Meaning that she can move between worlds and communicate with spirits on the metaphysical plane. A hedge witch is not only connected to nature but also to the spirits that exist along the thin lines of the veil.

An elemental witch focuses her magic on the four elements. Using earth, air, fire, and water to her will, this witch can connect deeply with the forces of nature.

Some elemental witches focus on a single element, while others might dabble in multiple.

Cosmic witches are attuned to astrology and the greater cosmos. They focus on birth charts and numerology and often enjoy discovering the mysterious connections between a person's life and their passions.

Sea witches are deeply connected to bodies of water, whether it be oceans, lakes, or rivers. They are often well-versed in magical sea creatures like the mermaid. Sea witches conduct rituals and spells under the light of the full moon as it sways and controls the tides.

An eclectic witch is one who combines many forms of witchcraft into her own and is one of the more common types of witches, as it allows a person to embrace different aspects of witchcraft and magical practice. An eclectic witch will enjoy astrology as much as the elements, and she enjoys herbal magic just as much as crystals, like the witch that this book is intended for.

THE CRYSTAL WITCH

A crystal witch is a person who incorporates crystals and gemstones into the many aspects of her witchcraft practice. She understands that each gemstone has a specific purpose and meaning, and she values those stones like nothing else. The energy residing within crystals and gemstones has untapped potential, and the crystal witch is well aware of this.

She will use crystals during her spells and rituals to enhance energy flow and bring about positive outcomes. During spells, the crystal witch will use her knowledge of the various types of crystals to create a powerful statement with her magic. This might be as simple as using clear quartz to amplify the other aspects of the spell and bolster the energy going into what the witch is manifesting. It can also be more elaborate, such as using kyanite to allow someone the ability to speak for themselves instead of feeling repressed and unable to voice their thoughts and opinions.

Although spellwork is powerful, they are not the only magical occurrence that witches use crystals for, especially not the crystal witch. An empowered witch knows that she must take special care to prevent energy overload on her physical form, mind, and spirit. This includes meditation, where a witch will sit with a specific crystal to either help raise her vibrations to pull together the right energy for an upcoming spell or to cleanse her body of excess energy after performing a spell.

The same can be said for therapy, which is at the heart of what many modern crystal witches focus on. Crystal therapy is incredibly powerful as it can help reduce stress and anxiety and is even known to remove depression and other unwanted feelings and thoughts. Crystal witches use their gemstones and crystals to help themselves as much as they help others so that they remain strong and can confidently continue their magical practice.

Witches that use crystals in their daily practice will often wear jewelry that contains the gemstones or crystals that are most dear to the witch, and they will often have numerous pieces of that jewelry so that they can change out their gemstones when needed. In addition, crystals can be used to create spell bags or spell jars that a person can keep hold of and use when seeking extra positive energy.

With crystals at the heart and soul of a crystal witch's practice, it isn't uncommon to find a crystal witch adorning her home with various beautiful crystals. These fantastic specimens can often convey powerful feelings and properties, such as an amethyst geode which can project feelings of tranquility and peace.

Even if you are new to crystal witchcraft and do not have a vast collection of beautiful specimens or exotic jewelry, just the mere fact that you are interested in crystals and drawn to them shows that you have already accepted the energy within you and are willing to work with it. These collections, just as much as the knowledge that comes from the practice of witchcraft, build over time. This slow but steady construction of our spirits gives us character and provides purpose in our lives as witches. Anyone can choose to take the path of a crystal witch, and along the way, some people learn to embrace various other aspects of witchcraft, making them an eclectic witch. Nonetheless, crystals and gemstones play a considerable part in the world of witchcraft, just as much as they do in the ever-changing world around us.

Magic is a free-flowing substance that some people cling to while others do not. When you realize that this is the path you should take, there is no turning back. You feel as though something has awakened in you, and you can no longer ignore it. Such is the call of nature and of that ancient energy we've already discussed. This is you, feeling that connection to everything—the animals, the trees, and of course, crystals.

With witchcraft, there are many pathways that a person can choose to continue learning and moving forward in their lives. One of those pathways is through the use of crystals. It's important in the beginning to know that labeling yourself as something specific is not necessary.

Defining who you are as you work to understand your true nature will not help you as much as it will for you to study and learn about the things you are drawn to. Such as crystals.

Modern witches, including crystal witches, come in different shapes and sizes. We are all a part of a unique group of beings capable of feeling and knowing things others may overlook. Witches are unique and have many distinctive personalities, and you might be surprised to find some people you already know are witches. This simply proves that labeling and stereotyping people does not define them. Your personal reasons for becoming a witch might be based on your religious background or a lack of one. It might also be because you were born into witchcraft or you have sought out the answers to the most basic questions we all have. Simply put, witches are everywhere, and we all have our reasons to want to build on our internal energy and empower our lives.

ONE FOOT IN FRONT OF THE OTHER

On the magical path that we are about to take, you and I will walk together as we enter the world of energy healing. In the following chapter, we continue on this path as crystal witches, joining together in the sisterhood of witchcraft. Now that we've laid out the groundwork, we can move into learning all about what energy is, how it works, and how we can harness it to perform magic. Here is where we begin our study into the world of energy and how our bodies are aligned with energy centers that can be cleansed and fortified. The wonderful benefits of energy healing await us!

2

ENERGY HEALING 101

*E*nergy is the basis of everything around us. It is within us, and in truth, it is us. Knowing how to feel the energy in our physical world is the first step in harnessing it and using it to heal. Energy is something that has always existed and will always exist in the greater cosmos. From the very early moments in the universe to the present day, energy has been the silent constructor of our reality.

Energy connects everything because everything is a product of energy. As Albert Einstein once said, "Reality is merely an illusion, although a very persistent one."[1] Einstein has long been admired as the father of physics, and his infamous equation of E equals MC squared will forever be etched in our minds. On its most basic level, this equation explains how energy and matter are interchangeable. Based on Einstein's theory of relativity, energy is equal to matter times the speed of light squared. In layman's terms, energy converts to matter, which means all matter has energy.

Diving deeper into physics, Einstein also suggested that two objects should affect one another's behavior even across vast distances. This is in the area of quantum mechanics, which states that even on the microscopic level, there is energy to be seen. Atoms hold specific energy sources, and electrons can only be found in certain energy states.

Energy and physics go hand in hand, and this discussion could get very scientific. However, for a crystal witch who is learning to find her own path through the use of energy work, the only important takeaway is to know that all matter contains energy. As I said before, this includes us.

HOW DOES ENERGY RELATE TO HEALING?

Now that we understand energy on a deeper level, we can look at the importance of its use in healing. Just as matter can change from energy and energy into matter, we can alter unhealthiness into healthiness. By taking the negative energy that is causing someone pain and moving it away from the person as we bring in positive and good-feeling energy, we begin the process of healing.

Healing is derived from the term haelan, which is the state of being whole. Hal, the root word, also translates to holy. Therefore, to make someone whole begins from deep within, nurturing the spirit first, allowing the body to heal in the physical plane. As Einstein said, reality is an illusion. More importantly, it is a construct of the energy of the universe that we have access to and can manipulate to change our perceived realities right before our very eyes.

This abstract healing that we are after, the one that helps us purify our spirits and become whole with the energy of the universe, is responsible for our emotions and our mental state. Furthermore, when we are hurting deep inside, we are suffering. The concept of suffering is at the heart of Buddhism, and only by obtaining enlightenment does one find freedom from pain, hunger, and disease. This enlightenment is not a miracle cure or some form of elixir that we can purchase. Instead, we have to put in the work to heal ourselves from the inside out. We must learn who we are and what we need from the universe to remove the bad energies and make way for good ones.

TO HEAL COMPLETELY IS TO UNDERSTAND SUFFERING

Healing takes part in our deepest conscience, and it does so by involving the spirit. We cannot heal unless we are to accept that something is broken. To accept this place of suffering, we must identify what it means to not be whole.

Thanks to Thomas R. Egnew's study, *The Meaning of Healing: Transcending Suffering,*[2] a new idea behind medicinal healing has emerged. Whereas, in the past, people attributed modern medicine to the effects of diagnosing and curing an array of illnesses and diseases, now we can look at healing as the transcendence of suffering.

In his study, Egnew found three main themes associated with the idea of healing. Wholeness represented the notion of needing to become whole again after an illness. This idea is unique as it assumes that a person must have been whole before the illness. This is simply an immeasurable subject, but it is evident that it goes beyond the physical and is related to the social and mental aspects of a person's well-being. Narrative was the second theme present in Egnew's study. It represents the life narrative that a person experiences throughout their lifetime. It intertwined with wholeness as people would continue on throughout their lives, wading back and forth between feelings of wholeness and the need to become whole again. Finally, spirituality was the third theme. It represents the intimacy in a person's life, the deeply rooted emotions and feelings that transcend the physical nature of the body itself.

Altogether, Egnew's study has demonstrated that the idea of healing is not simply a cure provided by a traditional doctor. It comes from years of building character as we learn to live with the illnesses that cause us suffering, rise above them, and move past them to become whole once again.

Thus, energy healing provides a bridge between living with and overcoming suffering and the illusions of the reality that we have constructed. Thanks to Einstein, we can analyze our reality through a different lens and apply it to Dr. Egnew's study to realize that we have the power to convert the energy around us into something positive that will allow us to rise above that which plagues us.

HEALING THROUGH ENERGY WORK IS NOTHING NEW

For thousands of years, practitioners of both medicine and spirituality have studied the effects of energy healing on the body. Whether it be a science that we have yet to understand or simply our minds bringing forth the reality that we wish to occur, energy work is a real and measurable solution to the many ailments we experience daily.

The energy centers throughout our bodies, also known as chakras, are each responsible for a specific duty within our metaphysical and physical beings. We will get a deeper look at these energy centers in the next chapter, so for now, let's discuss their history in the fields of medicine and spiritual healing.

Healing through energy, also referred to as energy medicine, has an intricate relationship within and throughout our physiological systems. The energetic interaction that energy medicine creates works directly with our bodies to promote homeostasis. When we speak of homeostasis, we refer to the steadiness that our bodies operate at to remain as living beings. Incorporating the effects of optimally functioning physiological systems and the rhythm at which we actively work to remain stable and alive, whether subconsciously or not.

This energy medicine stems from the idea that every person has a life force that culminates at certain centers throughout their bodies. A person's energy is then seen as vibrational energy, which emits constant energy just as much as it absorbs. This never-ending flow is what we deem as life, and when negative energies enter our living energy, we find ourselves in the midst of suffering.

We perform energy work to increase the positive energy and remove the negative from someone suffering. This is where crystals become incredibly important because, as mentioned before, some crystals can draw out unwanted energy and banish it from our bodies. Others can replenish our energy and bring us positivity by employing healthiness, happiness, and contentment.

Energy medicine, also referred to as vibrational medicine, is "based on the belief that the body is permeated by an energy field that can affect our health and well-being, also called subtle energy, vibrational energy, or simply life force." The statement was made by researchers in the 1980s, and it laid the groundwork for recognizing alternative medicines that encompassed mind-body medicine and energy healing.[3]

Modern scientific perspectives have utilized the idea of energy work as a means to explain life based on Einstein's paradigm. We, as humans, are made of a network of complex energy fields. This collective energy field often referred to as the biofield directly impacts our physiological state. What exactly does physiological mean in these applications?

When speaking about the physiological effects of the body, we are strictly referring to things such as the rate of oxygen that our bodies can take in, the pH balance of our blood, and the plasma deep in our bones. These examples are only a few compared to the many diverse physiological aspects of our physical bodies. And this is the root of our reality. Our organic, purely human bodies, which experience pain and decay, feel the effects of mental stress just as much as physical. And this is where crystals, yet again, can help cleanse our energies and remove the harm weighing down our physiological processes. Even something as simple as the shedding of dead skin is a physiological effect that our bodies may struggle with when we are suffering. With negative energy, we can find ourselves in a mix of unhappy symptoms that continue to pile up on each other because of our modern, demanding lifestyles.

Through the help of vibrational medicine, we can influence our energy fields to find balance and harmony.

This energy healing is available to everyone no matter what type of suffering they may be dealing with. Energy healing comes in many forms, and there are many diverse ways to implement these forms. Working with crystals in different forms is a way to create the vibrations necessary to heal holistically. Many of the methods can even be performed in the comfort of your own home. Crystals require little of us. You simply need the right crystal and the knowledge of what to expect from healing with crystals to find the right energy for a more positive way of life.

UNDERSTANDING YOUR OWN BIOFIELD

What exactly is meant by a biofield? We can think of this as an energy field that surrounds us, similar to how we view auras. With an aura, we see the different colors representing our energy as it leaves our bodies and lingers in the air around us. With a biofield, we are directly looking at this energy as it mingles with the other energies in our environment. This biofield is believed to be present simply because of our organic processes, which include the heartbeat and the lymphatic system, for example. Furthermore, according to scientific researcher and healer Mahendra Kumar Trivedi, this biofield is explainable due to neutrino oscillations.[4]

The Trivedi Effect is something Mr. Trivedi has developed and coined by using this biofield positively. By merely using his physical presence, or even intentions set forth by his thoughts, Mr. Trivedi has transformed certain characteristics and behaviors of both non-living materials and living creatures. His work has affected things such as plants, animals, and even metals. This goes to show that every piece of matter in the universe has energy residing within and around it. And thanks to the Trivedi Effect, we can analyze and identify how our intentions can change these energies at will.

What role does a neutrino play in all of this? Quite simply, neutrinos are subatomic particles that have, until recently, been very difficult to detect. They have little interaction with matter itself but are one of the most abundant particles throughout our vast universe. Trillions of neutrinos pass through matter, including our own bodies, every single day. After much research and the now accepted "standard model" of neutrino behavior, scientific researchers such as Mr. Trivedi can now hypothesize that the neutrino is responsible for aiding in the behavioral and characteristic changes brought on by intention.

While much of this becomes very scientific, on a most basic level, we can view the impact that a neutrino has on the biofield as a simple chemical reaction. For example, the human brain contains neutrinos and salt solutions. Based on the scientific experiments conducted by Frederick Reines and Clyde L. Cowan (the physicists who discovered the neutrino), neutrinos could interact directly with the protons of these salt solutions. This changes the salt on an atomic level, altering the neutrons, electrons, and other materials. Because the neutrino passes through matter, it can move from one person to another, thus invoking change. And this is but one example of potentially thousands of possible ways for the neutrino to create such change.

These heavily scientific studies have bridged the gap between western and eastern medicine, finally putting some science behind the energy work that practitioners have been doing for centuries. The groundbreaking scientific work that physicists have worked tirelessly to understand can now go hand in hand with the spiritual healing that our ancestors have perfected over millennia.

THE FACTS ABOUT ENERGY HEALING

When someone first hears about healing through energy work, they may be a little apprehensive, especially if it is a brand new topic to them. On the other hand, Witches are well-versed in the metaphysical and expect nothing less from nature. To denounce any uncertainties and clarify some of the myths behind energy healing, let's go over a few facts everyone should understand about healing through energy work.[5]

As we previously discussed, everything in the universe is made of energy, which often converts to matter. On an atomic level, the molecules within this matter vibrate at different frequencies, thus allowing for the transfer of energy. And again, neutrinos help to sway the energy flow from one thing to the next.

As I mentioned, with auras, we can visibly see our own energy fields and those of other people. While this might take a bit of practice, you can visibly see a person's suffering by identifying the energy field surrounding them. This energy field directly inter-twines with the physical body. Our thoughts can be made a reality, especially if we dwell on them for too long. Though abstract and distant, these thoughts can transpire into the physical world, bringing us pain and disease. Because energy work focuses on the abstract, the healing can occur on the biofield, which then trans-fers to the physical and heals the suffering.

Thanks to the groundbreaking work of Mr. Trivedi, we now know that energy work can be highly effective even when it only involves intentions. This is not a new concept, but it is now a proven one. With practices such as reiki treatments, a practitioner can transcend space and time to send healing vibrations to the person in need, proving that no matter who or where you are, healing is possible.

One of the most significant benefits of energy healing is that it is non-invasive. Energy work goes to the source of the issue and attempts to heal the deeply-rooted problem that is causing discomfort. This healing comes from removing blockages in the chakras and replenishing the body with good energy after a person has experienced sadness or trauma. Because healing can take place at any moment and in any situation, it is a quick and highly beneficial treatment option for those who need help and guidance immediately. Instead of waiting in long lines at a clinic or being scheduled weeks away to see your therapist or physician, wholesome crystal healing can be performed at a moment's notice.

Finally, it's important to note that healing through energy work, especially with crystals, can be done alongside seeing another doctor for your ailments. You might be on medication that you cannot give up, which is perfectly fine. The best part about energy medicine is that you can use it in tandem with western medicine to help relieve your symptoms as you work on healing your discomfort at the source.

Regarding suffering, our goal is not to cover up what is troubling us and pretend as though it never existed. This can lead to grief and depression. We must make it our aim to resolve the problems that are causing our suffering, whether physical, mental, or spiritual. When it comes to healing, the first step is learning to accept ourselves for who we are, pain and all. We must take this suffering and allow it to shape us in a positive way as we learn to move with the energies in and around us to fully heal and overcome the illnesses we wish to escape.

THE HISTORY BEHIND CRYSTAL HEALING

As far back as we can think, to the ancient civilizations that took hold and helped humanity flourish, crystals are adored for so many reasons. Not only were they beautiful and used in ornaments, but crystals also played a major part in rituals, medicine, and offerings to the gods during ancient times.

In the Creation Epic of Babylonia, the God Marduk would carry a red amulet to protect himself during battle. This tale comes from the seventh century BCE, one of many that speak of crystals holding sacred power. During the paleolithic era, people would use crystals for jewelry because of their believed magical properties.

And in modern times, Jacques and Pierre Curie, two French physicists from 1880, discovered that crystals emit an electrical charge when pressurized.[6] This is the same type of charge, called piezoelectricity, that both DNA and bones will exhibit. The ancient belief that crystals hold energy was finally confirmed for the first time.

It's no secret that we are all made up of the same matter that stars are made from. Just like the most gigantic objects in the universe, our bodies are made of elements. And with quantum physics, we know that everything is made from atomic particles. The elements that make up a human body include oxygen, hydrogen, and carbon, to name a few, which is also true for all other living and non-living things on Earth.

Even Nikola Tesla, a highly praised physicist who invented and engineered many groundbreaking ideas, understood that there was an energy residing throughout the universe that was shared amongst crystals. Tesla once remarked, "In a crystal, we have the clear evidence of the existence of a formative life principle, and though we cannot understand the life of a crystal, it is nonetheless a living being." Tesla was known to focus his efforts on the transfer of energy, and he was the first physicist who identified what we now call radiant energy, which is the basis for X-ray technology. This transfer of energy drove Tesla, and he spent a lot of his time working on transmitting power wirelessly across the city.

In our modern world, we are lucky enough to have this scientific research backing our beliefs. We've gotten to a point where we can understand on a scientific level just how the transfer of energy works, which validates our ancestors' beliefs about crystals. And it also confirms that each crystal can have its own metaphysical properties just in the way that we as humans exert our own energy fields in diverse and unique ways.

You may have noticed at some point in your life that being in a room with an angry person can often make you feel angry. That person's energy has transferred onto you, and you will then carry it around until you can also rid yourself of it. In the same respect, being around someone who is cheerful and pleasant will give you good feelings as you carry around a brighter and more positive emotion. Crystals do this same thing. Each one has a power of its own, and that power can lend itself to our bodies so that we can remove stress and feel better about ourselves. That is only the tip of the iceberg when it comes to all the incredible things that crystals can do.

At this point, a question you may be asking yourself is, if we can manipulate these energies, why do we suffer at all? The answer to this has everything to do with karma.

HOW KARMA ALLOWS US TO HEAL OUR SOULS

Karma is that magical force that keeps everything in the universe in line. We send good karma to receive it back. And when we create bad energy, that comes back just as well. Our misfortunes and traumas that caused us suffering are sometimes karmic wounds that we have carried with us from our previous lives. Until we learn to work through them, karma continues to make us aware that we have wronged someone or something, and we must atone.

Some spiritual teachings, such as Buddhism, view karma as a guiding principle to find ultimate peace. For the Buddhists, this peace is called Nirvana, and it occurs after your soul has enlightened and moved past all the suffering and negativity that you've carried throughout all your lives. The cycle of rebirth that you must endure to pay for your karmic debt is called samsara.[7]

In a new age of spirituality, often including witchcraft and neopaganism, people take the idea of karma to heart, as they should. Karma is directly related to the push and flow of the universal energy that we have been discussing in this chapter. Everything from the past, present, and future is already in existence, meaning that if you put out negative energy, it will most certainly come back to you. This means that the negativity you are holding onto has come from somewhere else, to begin with, but that is the balance of the universe. Where there is light, there must be darkness. Where there is justice, there must be injustice. These are things we cannot escape, and we must accept them and learn to move past them to heal.

Understanding our own karmic debt will allow us to repay the universe and even reap the rewards that we will learn from doing these good deeds. It isn't uncommon to carry around the extra weight of karma from our past lives, especially since we are so far in our human history that many of us are not in our first lives. We may be holding onto our past lives and the unfortunate events that occurred during them, even ones we caused ourselves.

As we move from life to life, we remain connected to certain people through karmic bonds, and sometimes these bonds mean that we share the pain and suffering from previous lives. If you have ever met someone and instantly thought that you have known them your whole life, this is a sign that your souls are already familiar. These bonds often come from being around the same people and the same souls time and time again. It is possible that our families, parents, and children alike come and go in our lives as we do in theirs time and again.

And the beauty of karma is that we are constantly creating new karma as we set forth intentions and take action toward things in our lives. Creating a balance in your karma by doing good things can bring forth new wonders in your own life, which can help heal the karmic debt accumulated in a previous life that you may be experiencing now.

While using crystals and energy work to mend our mental and physical bodies has an incredible impact, not knowing what karma is or how it works will leave you stuck in the same patterns. We need to not only be conscious of our actions and thoughts, but we must also actively seek an end to our suffering. Do not look at karma as though it is holding you back; it is simply the universe's way of keeping track of the deeds that have been done. We create our own karma, and that karma will allow us to heal fully, even within one life-time, if we are diligent.

Before using crystals to resolve our problems, we must first take a deeper look inside to ensure we are creating good karma for ourselves. Everyone has their own way of accomplishing this, and even the smallest gesture can reap big rewards. Once our thoughts and actions are aligned, crystal healing can truly take effect.

Let's take a closer look at the three types of karma and how they play into reincarnation.

Latent Karma (Sanchita)

With latent karma, we are talking about the amassed karma that your soul holds onto from past thoughts. This type of karma is just the beginning of something much larger in the future. We can liken it to a seed which will eventually grow into a flourishing plant. As you can imagine, if we plant a healthy seed and nurture that seed with kindness and compassion, our plant will grow strong and beautiful.

Ripened Karma (Prarabdha)

With ripened karma, we are talking about the karma that is happening to you now. Your previous actions and thoughts take hold of your reality. If the flowers of your plant are ample and fragrant, then your seed is good. If they are decaying and rotten, then the seed that you planted was bad.

Future Karma (Agami)

With future karma, we are talking about a new seed that you are currently planting. You now have a choice about what type of seed you wish to plant, whether it be good or bad. And now that you are experiencing the result of latent karma, you are able to discern which path is best for you. Of course, we know that no one likes bad karma to come along, so hopefully, those who are experiencing karmic misfortunes will have learned their lesson and aim to plant healthy seeds the next time around.

SELFLESSNESS IS KEY

When it comes to karma, and most especially karmic healing, learning to be selfless can free someone from their karmic debt. When we continuously focus on ourselves and allow others around us to continue to suffer when we are capable of helping them, then we are doing selfish acts, which creates bad karma. Continually focusing on oneself without ever pausing to put someone else first can cause great harm to the soul. And even if you have made great strides toward enlightenment, you can lose progress simply by living a life where you do little for others.

Our souls are eternal bodies of energy that, according to Hinduism, are all part of the divine force of the universe. When our souls stray too far from the divine, they lose their way and cannot find enlightenment.[8] This is when we get stuck in the cycle of rebirth and must reincarnate to continue to learn lessons and grow closer to the spirit.

We must remain aware of our intentions and actions if we wish to heal our bodies and minds from the inside out. This is especially true when carrying around karmic debt from past lives. Experiencing sluggishness and fatigue can be signs of karmic debt, and we must take these signs seriously if we ever wish to truly overcome our suffering.

HEALING WOUNDS TO IMPROVE KARMA AND REDUCE SUFFERING

Meditation is one of the many ways a person can clear their mind and allow for healing to begin. When we sit in meditation, we focus only on our breathing so that we can move past the physical stresses that weigh us down. Yet sitting in complete silence with only your thoughts can eventually wear on you, especially if you're dealing with old traumas. These may manifest as physical ailments, causing you pain and achiness. Mental stress can affect you just the same, causing headaches and fatigue.

Some of these stresses may arise from past karma, and one in particular often affects many people. This karma wound, known as a mother or father wound,[9] is a past trauma that leaves a noticeable amount of damage to the mind or body. And in truth, the mother wound is like no other. A person's relationship with their mother is all about the development we experience throughout our lives. With a nurturing and compassionate mother, our development can be a good one. But when we have unresolved feelings about things that did not go as we would have wished, we are often left wounded.

Like any other wound, the mother wound takes time to understand and reflect upon before someone can fully transform their viewpoint and heal. Working through your troubles with this all-important figure in your life is essential to finding peace and resolving the negative karma that may have come your way.

THE NEXT STEP ON YOUR PATH

With a more detailed understanding of the energy we use in crystal healing, where that energy is from, and how it is transmitted, we can now take a deeper look at the energy centers throughout our bodies. Understanding the chakras allows us to pinpoint exactly where our troubles are coming from. We can look at an issue we currently face and connect it to the exact energy source within our bodies where we may have a blockage.

Let's head into this next chapter to review and learn more about these energy centers and how they impact our everyday lives.

UNDERSTANDING CHAKRAS

*O*ur bodies are not only affected by the energy that passes over, but we also store and create energy ourselves. These simple facts of energy work are the building blocks for our internal energy centers, the chakras. These chakras are evenly spaced throughout our bodies and are directly connected to how we think and behave throughout our daily lives. In a moment, we will dive into the seven main chakras we can heal and focus on during energy work. But for now, let's establish a deeper understanding of how the energy flows throughout our bodies.

THE DIVINE CONNECTION

As we previously discussed, our bodies are made of energy, and that energy is directly connected to the divine spirit of the universe. This divine energy, which is pure and wholesome, feeds into us as much as it does the other living creatures across the cosmos. In addition, this energy is also found in nonliving things, like crystals and other stones.

The energy that gives us life comes from this divine source, which is why some spiritually based people, such as Buddhists and Hindus, are ever aware of the presence of karma in their lives. It is enlightenment that leads us back to the divine spirit in a never-ending state of euphoria. While we are here in this reality, however, we can continue connecting to this divine energy to heal ourselves and others if we wish.

As we go about our days, we experience different flows of energy in our environment. These contribute to the amount of energy and the type of energy that we store within our own energy centers. Not only that, depending on the energy we create by our actions and thoughts builds up inside of us in the same respect. When there is a constant flow of energy, we can transfer the negative energy out of our bodies and allow healthy energy to come in. But when there is a blockage, and our energy centers cannot release pent-up energy, especially when it is negative energy, we experience struggles and suffering both mentally and physically.

AN ENDLESS EXCHANGE OF ENERGY

Because our bodies are capable of storing energy just in the same way that they can absorb and release it, they are forever connected to the universe around us. There is a never-ending exchange between our physical bodies and our surroundings. Because of this, we can call upon or channel the divine energy of the universe and fill our chakras with the energy we need to perform whatever tasks we are working on. For some witches, this might mean healing with crystals through simple meditation, while others may focus on rituals and spell work. In either case, understanding the processes that involve energy movement and what it feels like when energy is coming and going through our bodies is essential.

You can think of this endless exchange as any other physical one you may have had in your life. Energy moves around us and through us at all times, even though we cannot see it. The key is that we can feel it if we pay close attention.

Imagine yourself laughing with your friends and how that happiness travels up through your body and seems to ease all of your troubles, even if for a brief moment. This shared energy that you have amongst people you love and cherish has brought you true happiness and contentment. It's more than merely finding something hilarious; this infectious laughter that you have with your friends is also because of the transfer of energy from one person to the next.

We all experience this daily and are so used to it that we have come to expect it without a second thought. We know that if we spend time with someone who is generally bitter and bothered, we already know that we will leave the situation feeling bothered ahead of time. Emotions and feelings are highly infectious, and it is because the person from whom the emotions originated has released that energy into the atmosphere around you. We all do this to each other, which is why we tend to connect with people who have similar thoughts and feelings about important topics. The last thing we want is to be around someone who constantly disagrees with us, especially on matters of high importance.

This energy transfer that we get from person to person is so prevalent because we are all full of energy, and we each draw and expel it on a regular basis. But the same is true for places and objects as well. For people who are highly sensitive, or for those who might be empaths, being in a building or an outdoor area that is full of good energy can make that person incredibly aware of the goodness that is seeping out of that environment. And the same is true for bad energy.

You may not have realized this, but there may be places that you tend to avoid simply because of the feelings and emotions you draw from that environment. Perhaps you favor a different grocery store that's a little further from home, or you tend to walk a certain way on your evening walk because you know that certain roads and neighborhoods feel better to be around. It might not have been your initial intention, but our subconscious mind knows exactly what it's doing.

Furthermore, because of the endless transfer of energy between people, their environments, and the objects that fill our vast world, these feelings you get can come and go and be altered by others who step into these places. The neighborhood that you choose to walk through feels the way it does because of the people who live there. But it goes beyond this. It is also the items that they keep, the actions that they perform, and the thoughts that they harbor. This transfer of energy from their bodies to their environment and then to you is a continuous flow. And people who choose to live positive lives often reap wonderful rewards and continue to do good. And if you remember, this is the core principle of karma.

THE CHAKRAS AS ENERGY CENTERS

There are more than a hundred chakras in the body, but here we will focus on the main seven that run along the length of the spine. Starting at the tailbone and going up to the crown of the head, these seven chakras each carry their own frequency and vibrational output.[1] Through the channeling that we do with the divine spirit, these chakras transfer energy by absorbing and releasing the energy that our bodies come in contact with. Everything about us impacts this energy as it flows throughout our bodies and into the world. Our behaviors, thoughts, emotions, and feelings all play a role in the energy that we give off. This is similar to how the energy from another person or an environment will come across as a particular type of energy based on that person's thoughts and behaviors.

Because our bodies are made up of energy, we must heal them with energy. This is the truest way to resolve pain and suffering. At the atomic level, energy transfer is constantly happening thanks to quantum physics and neutrinos. Healing with crystals is not only an ancient practice but is now verifiable through science. And to address each of the main chakras that are directly responsible for causing our ailments, we can select specific gemstones and crystals to heal from the inside out. Remember that the chakras can become blocked, and this blockage manifests itself through the physical and mental symptoms we experience.

To resolve the pain and suffering associated with blockages in our energy centers, we must first take a look at each chakra and what it is responsible for. Then we can understand what it means to have a balanced or an unbalanced chakra and how to treat it to resolve our problems.

THE SEVEN MAIN CHAKRAS

The seven main chakras that run down the spine are each responsible for something specific in our lives. Let's look at each chakra and identify what it is responsible for and how to determine if there is a blockage.

The Root Chakra

The root chakra sits at the very base of the spine, giving it the alternative name of the base chakra. This chakra is full of raw and primal energy that feeds our most basic instincts. It is the conduit for our energetic, metaphysical body that keeps us grounded in the physical world. It is associated with the colors red and black and the element of earth, which makes perfect sense because the element of earth is one of stability and physical security. It is these two that we seek out in our primal nature.

The root chakra enables us to survive. The root chakra is responsible for the kidneys, the bladder, the colon, muscles, lower extremities, and bones. When dealing with an unbalanced root chakra, we face fears involving our well-being, and we may be insecure or uncertain about our place in the world. Additionally, issues with the associated body parts, such as the kidneys, can also signify an unbalanced root chakra.

A blockage can also occur, which is more serious than simply having difficulties with the root chakra. A blockage is a buildup of energy that cannot be released, and that energy can feel toxic as it continues to vibrate within you with nowhere to go. Blockages may include any of the following physical or mental symptoms:

- Trouble with any of the associated body parts.
- Digestive discomfort
- Anemia
- Adrenal gland problems
- Depression or anxiety
- Paranoia
- Greed or resentment

- Low energy or the loss of interest in things that once pleased you.

The Sacral Chakra

The second primary chakra, the sacral chakra, is located about two inches under the belly button. This chakra connects with the color orange and is also related to the element of water. Like water, the sacral chakra is all about emotions, pleasure, and passion. This chakra connects with the lymphatic system and the reproductive organs. It is directly responsible for the sensations we receive from the world around us and our emotions, however deep and hidden they are.

When we have an imbalance with the sacral chakra, it will impact our intimacy and sexuality. It is, however, more than just physical attraction. This chakra is all about how we connect to other people through our relationships in this world. The sacral chakra also links to our creativity. When we have a low desire to express who we are or to find a creative passion as an outlet for our energy, we can experience instability in the sacral chakra. If you are facing a blockage in the sacral chakra, any of the following may occur:

- Infertility
- Sexual dysfunction

- Lack of confidence
- Attachment issues
- Addiction
- Emotional instability

The Solar Plexus Chakra

The solar plexus chakra is one that enables us to claim independence and confidence. This chakra is the third one in the body and is located in the upper abdomen. It connects with the color yellow and the element of fire. Just as fire burns bright and claims attention, the solar plexus chakra allows us to grow into our power as we transform under the will of our manifestations.

This solar plexus chakra is connected to the gallbladder, pancreas, and digestive system. This chakra is also representative of our personality. The energy that flows to and from the solar plexus chakra is often warm and bright, providing us with gratitude for what we have accomplished and the knowledge that responsibility comes with power. If there is a disruption of flow in the solar plexus chakra, any of the following may occur:

- Blood sugar issues and excessive weight gain
- Nausea and IBS
- Insomnia and lethargy
- Obsessiveness and perfectionism

- Low self-esteem and self-image
- Anger and frustration
- No motivation to care for oneself
- The inability to make decisions

The Heart Chakra

The fourth primary chakra, the heart chakra, is positioned directly over the heart. This chakra is connected with the colors green and pink and the element of air. The heart chakra is responsible for compassion, kindness, and generosity, to name a few. It also governs the lungs, upper extremities, the thymus gland, and the heart.

The heart chakra is the source of connection in our lives. This energy center is full of love and joy and is capable of showing us the most beautiful things in the world when properly balanced. Love is the purest form of medicine. When we are filled with love, we can heal and be healed. When our heart chakras are imbalanced, we can experience any of the following mental and physical ailments.

- Blood pressure or circulation problems
- Respiratory discomfort and illnesses
- Breast cancer
- Hatred, jealousy, or grief

- Manipulating others or feeling drained by toxic relationships
- Difficulty controlling your emotions
- Unwilling or unable to accept yourself or others as they are
- Isolating yourself or neglecting to nurture yourself

The Throat Chakra

The fifth primary chakra, the throat chakra, is found in the very center of the throat. As such, it's easy to understand how the throat chakra is associated with communication. It is also connected to the ears, nose, thyroid, and mouth. This entire area is all about expressing yourself with an authentic purpose as you learn to balance between the heart and the mind. The throat chakra aligns with the element of sound and the color blue.

The throat chakra allows us to speak of our beliefs and to stay true to ourselves without shying away from what other people might think. Words have power, and the words we choose to use, especially in a social environment, can give us strength. When experiencing an imbalanced throat chakra, however, we may have difficulties finding the right words as we struggle to identify what is true and what is not. Symptoms of throat chakra blockage may include the following:

- Throat issues such as head colds and laryngitis
- Earaches and tinnitus
- Teeth, jaw, or other mouth problems
- Speech impairments
- Being verbally aggressive or miscommunicating
- Judging people or being overly negative
- Apathy, arrogance, or insensitiveness
- Social anxiety or being shy
- Lying to or manipulating others

The Third Eye Chakra

The sixth primary chakra, the third eye chakra, is positioned between the eyebrows. This chakra is all about intuition and is associated with the colors indigo and purple and the element of extrasensory perception (ESP). This energy center guides our intelligence and our imagination. It is also connected to the brain, pineal gland, the eyes, and the pituitary gland. This chakra is representative of seeing beyond the physical plane to understand things on a metaphysical level, which is where clairvoyance and psychic senses come together.

When this chakra is full of healthy energy, flowing freely without any obstructions, we can reflect upon ourselves to understand our place in the vast universe. Our past mistakes and difficulties can teach us great lessons, and when we have a balanced third eye chakra, we can see these experiences as milestones on the path toward becoming our most authentic selves. When we aren't experiencing a balanced third eye chakra, our fears will take hold of us and stifle the visions that we have for ourselves. If you experience a blockage in your third eye chakra, any of the following may occur:

- Nightmares and sleep disorders
- Hormonal imbalances
- Headaches, clumsiness, and sinus issues
- The inability to learn something new
- Being fearful or close-minded
- Straying too far from reality and living within fantasy
- A disconnect from intuition and spiritual practices
- Fear of being critiqued or having to face change

The Crown Chakra

The seventh of the main chakras, the crown chakra, aligns with the spine, and the energy center is positioned directly at the top of the head. It is associated with the hypothalamus, the nervous system, and the skin. It is also connected to the colors of violet, white, and gold and is related to the elements of thought and light.

The crown chakra is all about enlightenment and our awareness of our position within the universe. It represents a connection to the spiritual realm, where we draw energy directly by raising our vibrations. With a balanced crown chakra, we can receive messages from our spirit guides through our divine connection at this energy center. When our crown chakra is not balanced, we experience a superior sense of self-worth that can be arrogant and motivate us to achieve material possessions instead of genuine connections with other souls. The following may occur when you experience a blockage in your crown chakra:

- Migraines and brain fog
- Neurological disorders, schizophrenia, and Alzheimer's disease
- Acne, light sensitivity, and eczema
- Entitlement, selfishness, and cynicism
- The inability to identify meaning in your life or to create goals
- Lack of deep relationships or being unable to trust others

- Feeling bored or that there is no inspiration or desire

How Crystals Heal the Chakras

When energy is blocked within our bodies, we must work quickly to enable that energy to flow freely, as it should. This is because every illness and disease begins within our energy centers and spreads as a way to handle the overload of toxic energy buildup. And when we let this energy build up go untreated, we experience suffering in a plethora of ways that only become compounded every day that we do not give it the treatment it deserves.

Crystals heal our chakras and allow the energy to be dispersed in the healthiest of ways because they can reactivate the steady flow of energy. Even when dealing with purely mental issues, such as anxiety and stress, crystals can help us work through these traumas to process what is bothering us. They allow for the negative energy to flow away from our bodies so that we can heal. One fundamental method for using crystals to heal our chakras is through meditation. With this practice, you can heal a blocked chakra in the privacy of your own home without the help of any practitioner. All you need is a specific crystal that can activate the chakra that you wish to work on. Let's go through the steps of this exercise.

First, we must choose crystals that are the same color as the chakras. For instance, the root chakra connects with the color red. We need to select a red crystal, such as red jasper, to use with our root chakra. Here are some examples of crystals with colors that align with each chakra:

- **Root**: Bloodstone, obsidian, onyx, red tiger's eye, and hematite.
- **Sacral**: Tiger's eye, carnelian, pyrite, and leopard skin jasper.
- **Solar Plexus**: Goldstone, rutilated quartz, yellow jasper, and citrine.
- **Heart**: Jade, unakite, rose quartz, green jasper, and rhodonite.
- **Throat**: Aquamarine, sodalite, lapis lazuli, and kyanite.
- **Third Eye**: Amethyst, ametrine, lepidolite, and blue apatite.
- **Crown**: Clear quartz, selenite, lodolite, labradorite, and serpentine.

After making your selections, you will need to find a quiet and comfortable place to lie down and relax. We begin by placing the crown chakra above the spot where you will lay your head. Once this stone is in place, you can lay down and begin placing the other stones onto the energy centers throughout your body. Each crystal will sit directly above the energy center that it corresponds with. For example, we will place a stone like rose quartz directly above the heart. Once you are finished placing your stones, you will lay still and meditate until you feel the energies vibrating rhythmically through your body.

This simple practice is great at getting the chakras aligned and flowing so that we can remove disturbances and ailments in their infancy. Doing this on a regular basis does wonders for your vibrational energy as a whole, and working on all the chakras simultaneously can stimulate this rhythmic flow. Still, if you are experiencing a particular blockage, you may want to give extra attention to that specific energy center. If you'd like, you can carry out this practice with a single energy center and any combination of chakras that need attention.

YOUR CRYSTAL JOURNEY AWAITS

Now that we have established a thorough understanding of chakras and how they filter energy throughout our bodies, we can take a deeper look at the crystals that will benefit us in our healing moving forward. Let's head into the next chapter, discussing which crystals are most beneficial and how to cleanse and charge them.

There are thousands of diverse crystals across the planet, each with its own healing powers. As we continue on this journey, remember that every person has their own path to walk upon, and each person is drawn to certain crystals for their own reasons. Even if you are facing a specific ailment and believe you need a particular crystal to help you, if you approach a display of different crystals and are drawn to one you didn't expect, do not ignore these feelings. This is your intuitive nature shining through and telling you that there is a reason you need the crystal that you are interested in. It's all part of the magic and power of nature!

4

HEALING CRYSTALS 101

*U*nderstanding the intricacies of how crystals can heal is not just scientific, as we have already examined, but it is also spiritual. This spiritual basis has carried on for centuries with our ancestors. The history of crystals most likely goes back to a time before we ever kept a written account. There truly is no telling how prevalent crystals have become in our evolution as human beings.

In this chapter, we'll briefly cover the history of crystal use throughout the major ancient civilizations. In addition, we will review how crystals work at clearing away toxic energy to allow for a healthy flow of positive energy that can transform and heal. And finally, this chapter will cover how to cleanse your crystals after

use and how to program them with your intentions so
that you can again use them to heal.

ANCIENT PRACTICES THAT SHAPED THE USE
OF CRYSTALS

Crystals have been used in various ancient civilizations
as far back as recorded history is concerned. For example, archaeologists have discovered fragments of crystals in the southern Maya lowlands, showing signs that
they were modified.[1] The presence of these crystals,
and the fact that they were altered for a specific use,
suggests that crystals were used in rituals. The Maya
civilization used their caves for various purposes, and
one of them may have included divination. This
suggests that these caves, and the artifacts found
within, held certain power to these people.

In Native American history, the teachings of crystal
healing have been passed on through word of mouth
for generations.[2] Native Americans have great respect
for the planet and everything that resides within and
upon it. This respect is not only for crystals but extends
to other forms of life, including animals and plants.
Native Americans believe there is spirit everywhere,
and by directly connecting with the Earth, they can heal
their spirits and bodies from the inside out.

The Indian Vedic texts give us another instance of ancient crystal use. In these ancient religious texts, we discover the origin story of crystals based on the Indian belief system of Hinduism. Through these texts, we get a better idea of why the people who follow Hinduism believe that certain crystals hold specific powers. For example, rubies are believed to be the blood of a demon named Vala, and this directly connects rubies to the physical nature of blood circulation and mental courage.

There is a deep connection between paganism and crystal healing that goes back to times before Christianity. In the ancient world, there was heavy reverence for astrology and the cosmos. And within this vast scheme, one that oversaw the balance between chaos and order, sat the Earth. In their eyes, pagans from the time before Christianity understood the connection of the spirit in everything, even though science would often oppose them. Observing the endless cycles of nature, these pagans connected crystals to planetary objects, behaviors of the gods and goddesses, and the seasons and the elements.

Even before people could explain what energy truly was, at least in the way that we now can understand it with the help of quantum physics and neutrinos, ancient civilizations understood that there was a vast network of liveliness tying everything together. Those people used their emotions and feelings about the natural world to identify the power hidden within crystals and later used those crystals to their advantage.

CRYSTALS ARE AN ALTERNATIVE MEANS TO PROMOTE HEALTH

Crystals are natural objects from the Earth, and as such, they can pull and hold untold amounts of energy from other natural bodies like the moon and the sun. These energies do wonders to our minds and bodies, raising our vibrations and lifting our moods like nothing else. Crystals can link our energy centers and channel individual energy into one to create this heightened vibrational state that moves energy from one place to the next. This is the basis for holistic and metaphysical healing with crystals.

While things in the metaphysical world aren't easily proven by scientific fact, at least not as quickly as our intuition can detect, we do know how energy works and how everything made from matter contains energy. This energy filters through the world and touches every inch of the landscape. Though we might not be able to explain this energy as it pertains to healing, not aside from the basic idea of energy transfer, we can analyze the results of using crystals to heal others. We can look deeper into what happens when people use crystals and to what extent healing has occurred. And through these results, we find that sometimes simply believing in crystals is enough to make a positive change in a person's life, even when it isn't your own.

HEALING THROUGH THE PLACEBO EFFECT

Sometimes all we need is reassurance that good things will happen to us, just like when we were little, and our mothers comfort us with something as simple as a warm glass of milk before bedtime.[3] While there might not be much scientific evidence supporting the idea that warm milk will help us fall asleep, it does indeed work for many people. And even as we grow up, we continue to use these nurturing experiences to our benefit.

This might just be an example of the placebo effect. Even though we like to imagine that everything will eventually be explained in time, some things may never have a reason for why they work. Some things simply do because we believe in them or because we believe in the person who is nurturing us.

Even for some people who do not believe in the meta-physical, or those who have doubts about holistic heal-ing, crystals can indeed heal simply because there is potential for healing to occur. If crystals did not heal in truth or on any basis that science could prove, then this would represent the greatest example of the placebo effect. Millions of people over millennia have used crystals for healing purposes, and they have been effective at healing because of their ability to transfer energy. But what if they couldn't transfer energy, and it was all just our belief in the magical idea that there was something capable of transformation sitting right here at our fingertips?

This is what the placebo effect is all about. When you put your trust in something, even if there's no reason to believe that it would work, and you achieve the outcome you were hoping to achieve, some scientists believe there is nothing more at work besides the placebo effect. But this is yet again another testimony to the incredible power of energy at work. Our minds focus so deeply on an idea, a possibility of obtaining something that would be dear to us, such as a healthy life, and we bring that idea into reality.

The placebo effect can also be applied to people who don't believe that crystals will work because if we, their support system and friends, reassure them that things will work out, it plants the seed in their minds that this is possible. This tiny hint of belief, even if in the friend and not the crystal, can turn into a flourishing transformation for the better.

RITUALS MAKE US STRONGER

We can take the placebo effect and the truth behind energy work to the next level by creating rituals that we consistently use in our daily and weekly practices. With rituals, even something as simple as a thirty-second prayer in the morning when you are about to leave your house, we create a consistent flow of energy that produces a constant reassurance for our psyches. In addition, we are creating a positive expectation of our future by enlisting energy work into our routines and working toward a daily goal with our affirmations and manifestations. This is known to increase dopamine, a neurotransmitter that makes us feel good about ourselves and gives us the desire to do the things that bring us happiness and pleasure.

Because of this, you can view the ritualistic practice of energy work and crystal use as the beginning of a nurturing and endless cycle of positivity. When we practice something that we believe could bring us a transformation toward the good things we seek, we remind ourselves of a future that we are actively working towards and getting closer to each day. And by keeping up with these practices, constantly reminding ourselves that we are doing what we can to reach the life we want to live, our brains reinforce this experience with dopamine to keep us happy and motivated. This is because dopamine is not only about feeling good but also plays a role in our memory and how we focus.

With all this information, where do we begin when it comes to healing ourselves and others with crystals? We must first understand the difference between crystals and other stones to get the right item for our energy work. Once this is accomplished, we can apply what we know to begin the true transformation of healing.

CRYSTALS, GEMSTONES, MINERALS, AND ROCKS

In the metaphysical world, the terms gemstone, crystal, and rock seem to go intertwined. While sometimes specimens will overlap these categories, each one has its own meaning and complexity. Certain things in our natural world may qualify as crystals, such as table salt, even though we wouldn't necessarily think of it that way. The distinction comes down to the internal molecular structure of each of these terms.

Crystals

With crystals, we have a completely solid material that is defined by a replicated molecular structure that is highly organized.[4] The elements that make up the crystal form patterns, and these patterns are reproduced millions of times over to grow the crystal itself. The growth of crystals is quite fascinating, as they must rely on first developing a nucleus that we sometimes consider a seed crystal. This is the very beginning of the growth of a new crystal, and once it attaches to a solid surface, the crystal can replicate its internal molecular structure.

Amethyst crystals, which are formed from quartz crystals, develop when a concentrated silicon dioxide solution becomes trapped within lava bubbles. Once the water portion evaporates, the remaining ions can form a crystal. Because there are tiny amounts of iron within the solution, amethyst develops a purple color. When we look at a geode, a solid rock containing crystalline growth, we can see how the crystal attached itself to the solid structure of the rock and then grew toward the center.

Gemstones

Gemstones are made from minerals cut from their raw state, then tumbled and polished. Raw gems are found in deposits throughout the Earth, and some of these deposits are finite. This produces a rarity of gemstones, and some that are difficult to find can be quite expensive. While crystal structures such as salt are commonly used on a daily basis, gemstones are often used as adornments in jewelry and decor.

Sapphire is a type of gemstone that forms due to pressure and extreme heat. Both metamorphic and igneous rocks can contain sapphires. A substance called corundum, which is within igneous rocks, may cool slowly enough to create large sapphire specimens. This, however, can take thousands of years to occur.

Minerals

With minerals, we are talking about pure elements or compound substances found across the planet and the cosmos. Minerals often form like crystals in how they replicate their internal structure and grow into precious materials. They are also created by geological processes like weathering, erosion, and natural events like earthquakes and volcanic eruptions. These processes are directly connected to the elements, such as wind erosion or flooding.

Rocks

A rock is an amalgam of different materials, most commonly sedimentary in nature. Rocks can contain minerals and even some remnants of crystals, but minerals are not considered rocks. You can think of rocks as a collection of diverse substances that have all come together over thousands of years to create a compound substance.

THE ENERGY OF A CRYSTAL OR GEMSTONE IS HIGHLY UNIQUE

The energy that a crystal or gemstone carries is all about how it was created. Gemstones forged through lava, like obsidian, react to our energy very differently than gemstones created through metamorphosis, such as tanzanite. The same is true for crystals, which have grown throughout the Earth for millennia under different conditions. Both gemstones and crystals have seen the Earth go through countless transitions of its own, and in all that time, they have patiently absorbed the residual natural energy around them.

During their formation, crystals not only take on this energy that has been lingering across the Earth and around them for centuries, but they also hold onto the stories of Earth's past, present, and future. When you pick up a gemstone or crystal, you can feel the energy coursing through it, and you can almost imagine where it came from and what it has seen during its life. This is,

again, another example of the transfer of energy that
we get from person to place to object.

Crystals can be formed by four different processes.[5]
During each of these, the crystalline structure is born
from the surrounding material and grows by endlessly
replicating its molecular composition. In some caves,
such as in Chihuahua, Mexico, crystals have grown to
be thirty-six feet long and over three feet thick. Under
the right conditions, crystals like these can continue to
grow perpetually.

Igneous Formations

Igneous gemstones are created deep in the Earth in
pools of lava. Some minerals associated with lava are
diamonds, peridots, and rubies. These gems form in
very high heat and are brought up to the surface by
volcanic explosions. Eventually, erosion uncovers them
entirely, which allows for their discovery.

Hydrothermal Formations

When a gem or crystal forms due to hydrothermal
processes, it is created in the depths of heated water. As
soon as the minerals within the water begin to cool,
they can crystallize and form visible gems and crystal
veins. Emeralds are created in this fashion, and it is
often the minerals of the surrounding rocks in which
the vein has occurred that can alter the color of the

crystals or gems. This is why some emeralds, for example, are lighter than others.

Metamorphic Formations

Perhaps the most common way a gemstone is created is by metamorphosis. During this process, different minerals become pressurized together, and due to intense heat and the movement of nearby tectonic plates, these minerals combine to create new substances. Some of them will even combine without having to melt. One common metamorphic rock is sapphire, and as we discussed earlier, sapphires are created in the intense heat and pressures deep within the Earth.

Sedimentary Formations

The fourth type of formation for gemstones and crystals involves sedimentation. In this process, particles mix with mineral-rich water during erosion and weathering, and this occurrence creates a new amalgam of gems. One example is opal, which is formed when water and silica mix together, and when that solution settles, the remaining silica spheres combine to create the opal.

NATURAL CRYSTAL SHAPES AND PATTERNS

Crystals come in various patterns and designs and can differ based on their composition and formation history.[6] The patterns include isometric, tetragonal, hexagonal, orthorhombic, monoclinic, and triclinic. Crystals grow into stunning designs that billow with the energy the larger they get.

Roughs

Great for spellwork, a rough gem is a natural rock formation composed of various minerals. These are the classic rocks that we all know, the igneous, metamorphic, and sedimentary rocks. The rough version of a rock is often what a gemstone turns into once it is polished and tumbled. Each one may look very similar to the next in its rough state, but when looking at the chemical and physical properties, they are all uniquely different.

Crystal Clusters

Clusters are stunning groupings of crystals that have grown together over time. Often, we find them growing on the surface of other rocks or within the hollow space of a geode. Clusters can be small enough to fit inside the palm of your hand, or they can be over a foot tall. These are great for energy healing because they contain many crystal points that can transmit large amounts of energy.

Crystal Points

The point of a crystal is the end piece that comes to a sharp tip. In geology, these points are called terminations. Any type of crystal may have a termination, and some have more than one. Many crystals obtain crystal points simply from natural processes like weathering. Some, however, may never have a point at all. These may be altered and polished to look more appealing, even if the point is artificial. Either way, crystal points are useful in energy healing as they are the point at which energy flow can be transferred and conducted.

Geodes

Gemstones and crystal geodes look like simple, common rocks on the outside. However, their inner core reveals a sparkling blend of mineral clusters once they are broken open. Geodes are beautiful centerpieces for home decor, with some small enough to be used in jewelry. Geodes are like little treasure chests that open to the magic of the natural world. Their raw energy is similar to the crystal cluster and can be used to cleanse and protect someone's personal space.

MAN-MADE CRYSTAL SHAPES

Some crystals are manually shaped so that they can serve different purposes for practitioners and witches alike. Even if the shape is altered, the gemstone or crystal retains every bit of energy it harbored from its original and raw state. Different shapes and sizes of stones are useful in their own way for the various things we do in energy work.

Tumbled Stones

The tumbled stone is perhaps the most common form of a man-made crystal or gemstone shape. A rock tumbler is a machine that moves the raw and rough stone around to polish it until it comes out shiny and smooth. People who are fascinated with gems and wish to polish their own stones can purchase a small rock tumbler for their own use. Rough stones can be tumbled in various sizes, bringing to light each rock's unique features and facets. These are often very accessible, small, and inexpensive, making them perfect for taking them with you on the go. They are also universal in use, applying to many types of spellwork like their rough counterparts.

Special Shapes

With precision tools and proper polishing, people can create gemstones to look like hearts, spheres, and eggs, to name a few. Each of these serves its own purpose, depending on the witch's desires. For example, stones that reflect compassion and romance are often shaped into heart shapes to further enhance the energy flowing through them.

Palm Stones

A palm stone is used primarily in meditation for a person to sit and hold onto a specific type of energy while they meditate. Palm stones are what you would think of them, flat discs that sit in the palm of your hand. Sometimes these are inscribed with sigils or meaningful words.

Wands

Some gemstones can be forged into wands for ritualistic and spellcasting purposes. Witches use wands when they are creating a circle or a sacred space. Typically, a witch will pick a gem that she is drawn to so that it holds extra power as she calls upon the spirits to guide her through the ritual. Wands are also great for cleansing a space or casting protection spells.

Pyramids

The pyramidal design has been around since ancient times and is thought to absorb energy through its base and emit it through the point at the top. Because of this, it is said that the pyramids in Egypt conducted massive amounts of energy for that civilization. Some healers who use crystals believe that the pyramid can open one's consciousness, allowing people to understand and cope with their difficulties much easier.

CHOOSING THE RIGHT CRYSTAL SHAPE FOR YOU

In the beginning, it can be difficult to choose a crystal shape that feels like it will do you the most benefit. There are hundreds of choices in common gemstones and crystals, and they all come in various shapes, sizes, and colors. This can be quite daunting as a beginner, but if you remain connected to your own energy and listen for your intuition to call out, you will easily find the right crystal shape for your practice.

The most important point to remember when seeking the right crystal shape is to pay attention to what is calling you. Even if you enter a metaphysical shop with the idea of purchasing a specific shape, you must keep your mind open to the possibilities before you. The universe and our spirit guides understand us on a deeper level connected with our subconscious and inner spirit. They can help to guide us and to show us the right path for where we are in our lives currently. This may go against everything you have expected when seeking out the shape you were looking for, but if you trust your intuition and listen to the voice inside, you'll discover the perfect fit for what you are truly needing.

Aside from the crystal itself, which is more important than the shape or the size, you can think about what you will be using it for initially to be sure that you get the right type of crystal. For example, if your goal is to make a collection of stones for chakra meditation, you may choose palm stones or small tumbled stones that you can use directly on your energy centers, as discussed in the previous chapter. Alternatively, if you wish to find an elaborate crystal to set on your night-stand to help protect you from nightmares, you may want to look for a geode or a similar crystal cluster in the crystal of your choice.

SIZE DOES MATTER, EVENTUALLY

As we move further into this book, we will go into more detail about what you're trying to accomplish and which crystals will help you the most. On that topic, the size of the crystal will matter depending on the purpose you have for it. For example, if you want a crystal to protect your home, you will want to choose one large enough so that the energy expands around the radius of your property. However, that probably won't be an option for most; instead, you can opt to have multiple smaller crystals placed in different spots around your home to enhance the vibrational protection that way.

Sometimes it's easier for us to use smaller stones in our energy work, especially when it pertains to the energy centers in the body. And as I mentioned earlier, meditation works especially well with palm stones and tumbled stones. Sometimes, however, we have a bigger project in mind, and we will need a larger, more capable stone to enhance the energies within us to make great things happen.

Now that we know more details about what crystals are, how they are formed, and how you might find the right crystal shape for yourself, we need to look at how to cleanse and charge our crystals to keep them strong and powerful.

HOW TO CLEANSE GEMSTONES AND CRYSTALS

Before we get into how we can cleanse our gems and crystals, we must understand why this is done. Firstly, we like to cleanse our gemstones and crystals when we first purchase them or receive them as gifts because they may have residual energy from the previous owner or the shop where they came from. Many people like to pick up and feel stones at these shops, and their collective energy can easily transfer onto the stone. It's always good to remove any energy that is not associated with you when bringing a new crystal or gem into your practice.

Secondly, when we repeatedly use our crystals, they offer us positivity as the transfer of energy moves from them to us. In this process, they often draw out negative energy from us and the environment. And even when they do not, they may become depleted from overuse or being away from their natural environment for prolonged periods of time. Just like how we have to replenish our bodies with wholesome foods and plenty of water every day, our gemstones and crystals require their own form of nutrition. And we do this by utilizing the natural environment.

Cleansing with the Elements

One of the simplest ways to cleanse a crystal and keep it strong is to use the elements of nature.[7] In each of the four elements, there are various ways that we can remove negative energy from our stones and allow them to absorb wholesome, positive energy from the universe. Utilizing nature is a beautiful way to imbue the stone with its natural energy by reconnecting it with its origin, the most natural source available.

Water is the most common element used when cleansing stones and crystals. You can leave your stone outside during a rain shower or simply rinse it under cool water. You never want to use boiling water or any water that is too hot to handle with your bare hands. In addition, some crystals and gemstones can break down when left in water for too long. Typically these stones are the ones that end in -ite. For example, labradorite is not the type of stone you want to leave soaking in water, but it can be briefly rinsed off.

Air is perhaps the simplest element to use in cleansing. You can leave your stones out in the wind or simply blow on them as you imbue positive energy onto them so that the negative energy falls away. In addition, you can use natural items such as leaves or feathers to wave wind and air across the stone to cleanse it.

Using the Earth can help ground the stone, pulling that energy away and into the Earth to be recycled and renewed. With this method, you can bury the stone or crystal outside in your garden overnight or gently place it on grains of sand. Again, like with water, some stones can be slightly more brittle than others. Make sure to be aware that more delicate stones may chip away when using dirt or sand as a cleansing method. Aside from dirt and sand, we can also use other earthly elements such as salt, rice, and healthy plants. For example, you can leave your crystal inside of your herb garden to allow the liveliness of flourishing plants to replenish its energy.

Fire is the final of the four elements we can use to cleanse a stone. With fire, you can pass the stone through the flame of a candle, or you can smoke the stone with incense if you wish. Whichever way, be sure that you are taking precautions so that you do not burn yourself. In addition, you can use a setup of three or four candles surrounding the gemstone as a symbolic cauldron.

Cleansing with the Sun and the Moon

Aside from using the elements, we can use the sun and the moon to cleanse and replenish our gemstones and crystals.[8] It's common practice for witches to use full moons to replenish and rejuvenate their gemstones and crystals. Simply leaving the stone under the full moon's light is enough to raise its vibrations and enhance its power.

The same is true for sunlight. Setting out your gemstones and crystals so that they can capture the light of the sun will invigorate them with renewed energy. This allows them to continue working optimally for us and in our healing and ritualistic ways.

You can even utilize a full twenty-four-hour cycle of moonlight and sunlight. The light of the moon, brightening the darkest parts of the night, is used to remove unwanted energies from the gemstone or crystal. Then, as the day renews and the sun rises, the crystal becomes awakened with fresh energy and warmth. Beware that some stones will get brittle and crack or even fade in color when left in the sunlight for too long, often more than a couple of hours. If this does happen, no significant energy will be lost, and you will still be able to take advantage of the crystal's powers.

It's important to note that even with heavy cloud coverage, the sunlight and moonlight will shine through and impact the stones just the same. And if you find your crystals have been left out under a cloudy night as it begins to rain, this is a bonus that allows you to utilize multiple cleansing methods in one go!

Cleansing with Other Crystals

The third most common method for cleansing crystals is using other crystals that are known to remove energy and raise vibrations wholesomely. Quartz crystal is perhaps the most popular. You can use a larger quartz crystal than the crystal you need to cleanse. You can also use multiple smaller quartz crystals simply and place them together in a bowl or on your altar. The objective here is to bask the crystal in the quartz's cleansing presence. This method works well when combined with the elemental method, as you can smoke the stones with incense or leave them under the light of the moon.

Raising Vibrations with Corresponding Cleansing

All gemstones and crystals have correspondences, just like how our energy centers connect to specific colors. For example, moonstone is connected to the moon and, as such, is also connected to the element of water. Because of this, moonstone can be cleansed under the light of the moon and also with the element of water to increase the vibrational output and restore it to its highest level.

You can think about these correspondences when it comes to cleansing your own stones and crystals, and choosing the right element or method of cleansing may have a lasting positive influence over your future energy work.

Cleansing For the Long Term

With so many methods at your fingertips, choosing one (or a few) may be a daunting task for beginners. My recommendation is to start with what you have available and what you are comfortable with. Afterward, you can experiment to see what works best for you and your own practice.

Depending on how often and intense your spellwork is, your cleansing frequency could vary. I recommend conducting a cleanse at least once a month. However, you must pay attention to how the crystal feels physically and energetically; this will help you determine how often they need to be cleansed. You will be able to gauge the status of your crystal through this feeling. Perhaps your crystal may emit a dark, heavy, or fatigued energy, which is a good sign that it's time to cleanse. When your crystal feels energetically lighter, brighter, and uplifting, it is ready for the next step, programming.

PROGRAMMING YOUR CLEANSED CRYSTALS

Now that we've cleansed our crystals, we can program them to be used specifically with our intentions.

Programming our crystals allows us to put our thoughts and intentions into the crystal so that it has a purpose. Because our minds and our bodies are intricately connected, our intentions are communicated to our physical cells through our energy fields. We then transfer this energy into the crystal so that it knows exactly what we expect of it and how we'd like to use it.[9]

Not only does this give the crystal purpose, but it also creates a bond between our bodies and the crystal. We will be deeply connected to the crystal now, which is why it's so important to cleanse it when it first comes into our lives. Having residual energy from another owner or from the shop where it was on display can alter its purpose. When this happens, the crystal does not act as effectively as we need it to, and healing can take longer.

When we speak of intentions, we align our desires with that of the crystal. For example, if I have a clear quartz crystal and my intention is to use it to purify nearby crystals and amplify their energy, then I would meditate and work with visualization techniques to program the clear quartz crystal with the purpose and intent of cleansing other crystals and raising their vibrations. This can be done with any crystal, and each one can assist with multiple things to help us heal and guide us as we empower ourselves in our own lives. Because of this, we must be clear with our intentions to align our energy with our crystals and communicate exactly what we are trying to achieve.

Anytime that we feel our crystals are not working as intended, we can cleanse them again to remove excessive energies that are unwanted and are serving no purpose. Crystals need to be cleansed periodically, even if they are only handled by ourselves. This is because they have done their work and are now full of energies we would like to dispel. In addition, some crystals need to be replenished by nature and the elements simply because they are depleted of energy.

We can program our crystals in many ways, but the most basic and easiest to follow is by meditating with our cleansed crystal as we bond with it and set our intentions.[10] Let's go over this method step by step so that you can easily program your crystals and have confidence that they will work alongside you towards your goals.

Meditative Crystal Programming

Firstly, we must find a quiet place where we feel comfortable and safe. It's important to be somewhere you are familiar with that makes you feel like yourself. You won't want any disturbances during this meditation because those can influence your intentions. If you are suddenly frightened by a loud noise in the environment that you pick, that fear can go into the crystal quite easily. I personally like to sit in my room in the early morning or late evening when the house is calm. I turn off all devices and close my door, so I can be left completely alone. If you become distracted or have interruptions, don't fret. You can cleanse your stone again so that any energies that have entered it during your meditation will be removed, and then you can proceed to meditate once again.

Secondly, you will want to hold your cleansed crystal in front of you so that you can see it clearly. This allows you to create a solid connection with your crystal as you begin the bonding process. Take a moment to feel its native and raw energy as it seeps out into your hands. This energy will mix with your own as you continue to cradle the crystal. Keeping the crystal in your eyesight, you are now connecting on a molecular level with your crystal.

Thirdly, focus on precisely what you hope to achieve through this crystal. This is your intention. You should have a vivid image in your mind of what you hope to get from using this crystal in your daily practice. For example, if you wish to alleviate digestive issues, visualize yourself being happy and content after eating a meal that would often cause you discomfort. As you stare deeper into the crystal, let this vision take hold of your mind's eye. This intention travels from your thoughts to your body, to the crystal through your touch and your visualization as you continue to stare.

Lastly, and most importantly, you must allow yourself to feel this energy coursing from your thoughts through to your fingertips and into the crystal as you continue to hold tight to that vision of yourself you are hoping to achieve. The more specific you are, the more the crystal will understand and bond with you, helping you manifest the outcome you are hoping for. As you do this, you can include mantras or words of encouragement to reinforce your intention. In this example, you can make a statement as you feel that energy transferring from you into the crystal, all the while keeping your vision locked in. Say out loud, "I will feel good after eating. I will not let food hinder me."

If at any time you feel like you've lost sight of your vision or cannot feel that energy transfer between your body and the crystal, you can repeat this process until that stability you are searching for is there. Continue to dig deep, bond with this crystal as you speak, and visualize your intentions with as much detail as possible. Remember that the clearer you are with your intentions, the more likely they are to come true.

MOVING FORWARD ON YOUR PATH

In this chapter, we have reviewed so many wonderful ways to cleanse and program our crystals so that they can work exactly how we wish. This deep connection with your crystals is almost like making a new friend. You will now have a sturdy companion that you can carry in your pocket or put on a necklace so that you will always be able to manifest those intentions you have set forth.

Now that we understand these basics of working with crystals, we can look at the most common ones that will help you build your own useful and prosperous collection. In the following chapter, we will look at thirty-four specific crystals that can do a plethora of things to help improve your life and empower your practice.

5

34 CRYSTALS FOR BUILDING OUT YOUR CRYSTAL COLLECTION

Of the thousands of diverse crystals available across our planet, this chapter focuses on the thirty-four most common ones that witches like to use. These are typically easily accessible and are not too costly, so you can begin building your collection in no time. There are a few topics we should go over before you start seeking out crystals to add to your collection. These topics will help ensure that you choose the best crystals for yourself while supporting the planet and those who work tirelessly to get us these amazing crystals.

WHERE TO FIND CRYSTALS

There are a few different places to discover new crystals, such as metaphysical shops, both online and in person, and even when you're out taking a walk. Some states and nature parks are more prone to specific crystals than others, but finding one yourself might be a sign that it will be helpful in your life. In addition, some yearly festivals and fairs cater to the metaphysical world. You can easily find new crystals in those places, both in their raw form, tumbled and shaped. Some noteworthy festivals and fairs may include psychic fairs, Native American gatherings, and mineral and fossil shows.

There are countless crystals available on the internet. Still, you always want to be careful to choose a reputable source that will provide good quality crystals for a reasonable price. Choosing crystals online can be a little tricky if you aren't sure what you're looking for because you aren't able to hold them in your hand until it ships to your home. For this reason, it's wise to choose a retailer that will allow you to exchange or return your item if it isn't a good fit.

Metaphysical shops are perhaps the most common for finding new crystals. These shops are also called new age shops and don't only cater to witchcraft and paganism; sometimes, it is just the new age movement that draws people in. These types of shops often have a good variety of various crystal sizes and shapes, and they are also known for selling things like incense, sage sticks, clothing and handbags, and art. The new age movement of the past couple of decades has helped these shops grow in popularity, and most major cities will have a couple to choose from in the least. Going to a metaphysical shop is nice because you get to hold and examine the crystals in person before making a purchase. This allows you to connect with the energy of the crystal, but also be wary that other people have handled the crystal as well.

CHOOSING ETHICALLY SOURCED CRYSTALS

While you are out shopping, it's always best to ask the shop owner if the crystals are sourced in an ethical manner. Some places on the planet do not source their gemstones and crystals ethically, which means that even though these crystals can create so much good in the world, the way that they are mined is done in such a negative way that it can lead to bad energies lingering in the crystal. Sometimes people are not treated fairly or appropriately paid in certain minds, which can cause an energy build-up that might remain with the crystal and damper your intentions. Of course, we can still cleanse these types of crystals, but it may take a little more effort, and it still doesn't do anything to lessen the harm done in the process of mining the crystal in the first place.

To determine if your crystals are ethically sourced before you purchase, you can ask the shop owner these questions. This goes for online and in-person shops, and people at festivals and fairs should also know the answers to these questions.

> *Are the people who mine for these crystals paid fairly?*
> *What are the working conditions like for them, and are these people safe as they work?*
> *What is the environmental impact of where these crystals are sourced?*
> *Does the mine use child labor to obtain the crystals?*

These are a few of the questions you can ask the shop owner, and if you have any other concerns, typically, the shop will be happy to assist you. Many witches and new age practitioners are very concerned with the environmental impact of mining crystals and fair labor across the planet. Some of the crystals that you will find, come from places with clear laws and codes of conduct, such as within the United States. Other places, however, are a little more vague about these topics, and it may not be easy to get clear answers to your questions when gemstones and crystals come from those places.

Part of working with nature is to become in tune with nature; by doing this, we feel the highs and lows associated with everything the cosmos goes through. When things are sad or unfortunate, such as when crystal mines are being unfair with labor pay and the conditions are unsafe for those workers, we can feel that impact in the palm of our hands as we hold that crystal. We want to be mindful of everything we do with nature and to be grateful for what nature has given us.

TAKE YOUR TIME TO BUILD YOUR COLLECTION

It may be tempting to purchase all kinds of crystals and gemstones that you encounter, especially when you get to see them up close. Their intricate patterns and natural beauty are hard to pass up, but we must take our time as we build our crystal collection. Purchasing too many crystals at once means that there may be a good chance you push a few aside and not use them to their full potential. Those crystals will have little purpose for quite some time and may sit around and become neglected. This energy can be cleansed, but it might be overpowering for a new witch to go through and cleanse and program a bunch of crystals at one time just to prevent energy decay.

Instead, you should focus on bringing one or a couple of crystals into your life and home at a time so that you can fully bond with them and program them with your intentions without feeling rushed. As I said, it can be exciting to go through many types of crystals and gemstones, but it may be overwhelming to have so many sitting there, waiting for your attention.

Like anything you bring into your practice, you will want to allow yourself plenty of time to connect with the new crystal so that the bond you make can be lasting and full of positive benefits. In my experience, I will often go out in search of a new crystal for a specific ritual or spell that I have in mind. Or even if I am in the mood to craft a new piece of jewelry to work specifically on an energy center that I feel needs my attention. Typically, in doing this, I will often run into a couple of other crystals that grab my attention. This means I may purchase two to three crystals at a time, but it isn't a regular occurrence. I wait until I feel the need to seek out a particular crystal for my work, and then I allow myself to browse and keep myself open to the possibilities that another crystal may be calling me.

THE MOST NECESSARY AND HELPFUL
THIRTY-FOUR CRYSTALS FOR ANY
COLLECTION

Now that we have all the basics out of the way, we can
focus on the thirty-four crystals that will help to create
the basis of your core collection. You can find these
crystals in almost any shop, and they are available in
different sizes and shapes. Here, we will also speak
about the many uses that each crystal has, a bit of
history, and how to identify the crystal itself. By the
end of this chapter, you will be well-versed in the main
crystals and what they are capable of doing for your
health and your magical practice.

Amazonite

With a vitreous luster and triclinic crystal pattern,
Amazonite is a stunning crystal found in purple, blue,
and green.[1] This crystal is nicknamed the "hope stone,"
and as such, it provides positivity for the person
holding or wearing it. The history of Amazonites goes
back to the Amazonian warrior princesses, to which
the crystal is rumored to have lined their shields.
Amazonite was also found throughout the temples of
Tutankhamun, and it is associated with the Book of the
Dead. This crystal brings a soothing atmosphere to the

home and can provide calmness when worn as jewelry. It can easily be cleansed with a quick rinse.

Healing Properties

- Relaxes us from anxiety and stress
- Clarifies thoughts on making smarter choices
- Connects to the throat chakra and heals thyroid issues
- Brings wisdom and intelligence

Amethyst

Amethyst is a type of quartz with an eye-catching purple hue that can sometimes be glasslike.[2] Amethyst has been a part of major civilizations as far back as 25,000 BC. Almost everyone from the ancient world, including Egyptians, Romans, and Greeks, adored amethyst. It can be used in meditation and also worn as jewelry to invoke peacefulness in your life. Because it is associated with higher spirituality, amethyst can be cleansed by using sound. Do not leave amethyst in direct sunlight, as it can fade dramatically.

Healing Properties

- Grants wisdom and higher knowledge
- Aids in better sleep and pleasant dreams

- Removes negative thoughts to allow for better decisions
- Aligns with both the crown and third eye chakra
- Adds a calming sense of spiritual peace
- Connects the real and tangible world to the abstract of the divine

Angelite

Angelite is a beautiful, powdery blue-colored crystal. As a type of gypsum, angelite forms after millions of years when Celestite is left compressed deep in the Earth.[3] Because this crystal is soft and delicate, it can easily absorb moisture and must be cleansed in ways that do not involve water, such as surrounding it with clear quartz in a small bowl. Angelite has an ethereal quality to it and, as such, has played a big role in the mysticism of Peru. Adding this crystal to your jewelry can help open your spiritual self to the messages the universe sends you.

Healing Properties

- Heals the throat chakra and thyroid
- Resolves pent-up anger and frustration
- Relieves toxic emotions from past traumas

- Adds tranquil and whimsical vibes to the environment

Aquamarine

With hexagonal crystal patterns and a beautiful vitreous luster, aquamarine is an ever-popular crystal of choice.[4] This crystal comes from the mineral beryl and can be anywhere from soft and pale to bold and vibrant blue. Aquamarine is nicknamed the "mermaid stone" because it is believed that this crystal was once a part of the ocean that had been turned into stone. It is calming and yet mysterious, and for centuries people along the coast would carry aquamarines to protect them from possibly drowning. To cleanse an aquamarine, simply rinse it through water, but avoid hot temperatures as it can react with thermal shock. You'll also want to avoid leaving it in direct sunlight for more than a couple of hours; otherwise, the color may fade.

Healing Properties

- Connects to the throat chakra
- Balances allergies and hormonal difficulties
- Calms emotions and provides clarity
- Enables us to speak our truth and be expressive

Black Obsidian

Obsidian is a type of crystal that forms after felsic lava cools rapidly.[5] It has a beautifully reflective surface that occurs naturally in black, but there are varieties with different colors and patterns as well. This crystal is great for grounding because it holds such raw energy from deep within the fiery pits of volcanoes. Evidence shows that the Mayans used obsidian for trading as early as 100 BC. In addition, obsidian is also found throughout the ancient world in Greece and Iceland. We can use obsidian in jewelry and as ornaments in our homes to keep us grounded and protected against negativity. Obsidian should not be left in sunlight or water for too long as it can make the stone brittle.

Healing Properties

- Connects to the root chakra
- Binds our bodies to the physical nature of reality
- Enhances courage
- Increases circulation

Black Tourmaline

Black tourmaline is a member of the extensive tourmaline family of crystals, which are silicates and have trigonal crystal patterns.[6] This crystal is excellent at protecting against, banishing, and absorbing negative energy. Much like a black hole, black tourmaline eats up the negative and unwanted energy surrounding you, and before long, you feel as though those energies never existed at all. Wearing this crystal or keeping a raw specimen of it in your home can filter out negative vibes and enhance confidence at the same time. Tourmaline can purify itself, but cleansing it with a rinse or under the moonlight is just fine.

Healing Properties

- Connects to and heals the root chakra
- Can help boost metabolism
- Dissolves anxiety and removes worry
- Enhances confidence and provides clarity
- Protects against Electromagnetic Fields (EMFs), which is highly beneficial for empaths

Bloodstone

Bloodstone is a beautiful, deeply colored green crystal with specks of red throughout.[7] It is a type of chalcedony that sometimes goes by the name heliotrope. This crystal is very high in iron, and due to its unique appearance, the name bloodstone is perfectly fitting. This crystal is all about the raw energy of our physical nature as humans, such as survival, instinct, and sexuality, and wearing jewelry with bloodstones will enhance these properties. This crystal can be bathed in lukewarm salt water and left to air dry.

Healing Properties

- Connects to the three lower chakras
- Creates physical strength and vitality
- Helps with illnesses associated with blood
- Assists women during their menstrual cycle
- Creates a sense of self-worth
- Grounds us to and aids in success with the material world

Blue Kyanite

Blue kyanite is a dreamy and visually pleasing mineral that is typically found in quartz.[8] It can come in orange, green, and black, but the blue version is the most well-known and favored. It has a triclinic crystal pattern, and most specimens resemble a bright blue sky with streaks of white clouds. Kyanite is a stone of truth and restoration, vibrating at high energies that can provide communication and healing for the throat chakra. As a stone of water element, kyanite does best to be cleansed under cool water, but do not leave it soaking. The iron within kyanite can rust if you do, altering the color dramatically.

Healing Properties

- Heal the throat chakra
- Allows for truth and honesty
- Creates new neural pathways to overcome trauma
- Resolve stress and sadness
- Strengthens third eye chakra to create clarity
- Build harmony in relationships

Blue Lace Agate

Blue lace agate is a combination of quartz and chalcedony.[9] Even though agates come in many colors and varieties, blue lace is a delicate, powdery blue crystal that enables positive communication in all directions. This crystal can be placed in the home to create a calming atmosphere, and when worn as jewelry, it allows us to gracefully stay true to ourselves. To purify and charge your blue lace agate, simply leave it under the light of the moon.

Healing Properties

- Clears throat chakra
- Heals the bridge between our hearts and minds
- Enhances self-expression
- Enables communication

- Creates a carefree and spiritual atmosphere

Carnelian

Carnelian, also called the "sunset stone" by many, is a brilliantly colored orange stone with a hexagonal crystal pattern.[10] Because of its color, carnelian is known for creativity and bountiful energy. This crystal provides the wearer with confidence and inner power, which is why it has been used throughout history by warriors going into battle. This crystal can be placed in the home to create inspiration and energy, and it can be cleansed with simple soapy water and a soft towel.

Healing Properties

- Inspiring creativity
- Empowering physical energy
- Connecting to the lower chakras
- Invoking safety and connectivity to the Earth
- Creating passion and intimacy

Celestite

Celestite is a dreamy stone made from strontium sulfate.[11] It exhibits colors of pale blue, pink, green, and white. This crystal is all about dreamy vibes and connecting with spiritual realms. This crystal is found all across the globe in exotic places like Egypt and Peru and in European countries. We can add this crystal to the home or office to increase communication and create a soothing and peaceful environment. For jewelry, Celestite offers clarity and patience. This crystal does best being cleansed by moonlight, but if we leave it in the sunlight, the color may fade or become altered. Avoid cleansing this stone with water, as it can dissolve.

Healing Properties

- Cleanses and grounds the chakras
- Clears out and refreshes the aura
- Creates inner balance and peacefulness
- Work with upper chakras to expand wisdom
- Creates clarity with the spirit realm

Chrysocolla

Chrysocolla is an opaque blueish-green crystal made up of various different gemstones.[12] Its high copper content gives it speckles of a bronze color throughout. Chrysocolla comes from two Greek words, *Chrysos*, which means gold, and *Kola*, which means glue, And it gets this name from being one of the first items that goldsmiths would use to weld metals together. Also called "The Eilat Stone," it is rumored to be mined from Africa in King Solomon's mines. Chrysocolla brings positive energy to the home, and when worn in jewelry, this crystal sends high vibrations to every inch of your body. You can use smoke to cleanse chrysocolla, but avoid using water, and do not submerge the stone as that can make it brittle.

Healing Properties

- May help lower blood pressure and regulate blood sugar
- Soothes nerves and removes anxiety
- Raises self-confidence and inner positivity
- Helps us communicate and remain mindful of others
- Connects the throat chakra to the heart chakra

Citrine

Citrine is a lovely bright stone that is often called "The Sunshine Stone." It comes from all over the world, in places like Russia, Madagascar, Scotland, and Brazil.[13] Ancient Greeks used citrine as a decoration item as far back as 300 BC. Keep citrine in your home to increase luck and positivity, and wear it as jewelry to instantly elevate your mood. We can cleanse this crystal with water or a bit of sunlight but do not leave it in direct sunlight for more than a couple hours as the color can fade.

Healing Properties

- Adds warm, sunny vibes to any situation
- Helps heal the thyroid, enhances circulation, and soothes the skin
- Fights chronic fatigue and brings about extra energy
- Releases tension and allows us to happily move past what is holding us down
- Connects to the solar plexus chakra and the sacral chakra
- Raises self-esteem and gives us personal power

Clear Quartz

Clear quartz, also called rock crystal, is perhaps the most common and versatile crystal used in witchcraft. It is a mineral composed of silicon and oxygen atoms with a trigonal crystal pattern.[14] Some specimens are transparent, while others are frosty white. Using clear quartz in your home brings a cleansing and healing energy, and when worn in jewelry, clear quartz can enable a peaceful flow of energy. We can cleanse and charge clear quartz under the light of the moon, and it does well in water, but rough specimens should be handled with care. Any type of quartz cannot be left in direct sunlight because it can fade easily.

Healing Properties

- Amplifies all other stones
- A master cleanser and universal healer
- Helps the immune system and clears away toxins
- Wards off negative energy
- Connects to all energy centers
- Nurture spiritual growth

Fluorite

Fluorite, a halide mineral, is a crystal that comes in many colors, most especially those with transparency, and it has a cubic crystal pattern.[15] It is found all across the globe in tropical places such as Mexico and Brazil and is commonly known as the "genius stone" for its ability to clear the mind of confusion. Because fluorite comes in so many colors, choosing one based on that color's properties can bring everything from luck to joyfulness into your life. This crystal shouldn't be submerged in water or cleansed in sunlight as that can leave it brittle and worn down. Instead, opt for cleansing and charging fluorite under the moonlight.

Healing Properties

- Purify the body and aid in overall health

- Remove toxins and negative behaviors
- Assists with bone and joint troubles, most especially arthritis
- Increases self-assurance and clarity
- Stimulates creativity while keeping you grounded
- Encourages optimism to move beyond past traumas

Green Aventurine

Aventurine is a type of quartz that sometimes comes in red, orange, blue, and brown. The most common form is green, and the shimmering luster of the stone is known as aventurescence.[16] Green aventurine is found throughout India, the Amazon jungle, and Russia. Because it is a green stone, it is connected with fortune and femininity. Wearing aventurine in jewelry can bring extra bouts of good luck and help the wearer to take charge when necessary. Aventurine does best when being cleansed or charged surrounded by healthy plants. This crystal does not do well when left in the sun or submerged in water for too long.

Healing Properties

- Brings balance to the nerves
- Assists with fertility

- Enhances positivity
- Encourages abundance
- Removes blockages in the heart chakra

Green Jade

Jade is often found throughout East Asian culture, and even though it comes in a variety of colors, green is the most adored and used version.[17] In China, jade is often celebrated but is also used in places like Spain and New Zealand. Some ancient people would call jade the "dream stone" because of how it can connect to higher realms and the dreams of the wearer. Keeping jade in your home or office will attract luck and bountiful prosperity, and it is also known to purify and bring harmony to the environment.

Healing Properties

- Balances bodily systems such as the bladder, the kidneys, and the spleen
- Awakens the libido
- Raises self-esteem and brings about confidence
- Enhances the heart chakra and invokes compassion and trust

Hematite

Hematite is a metallic stone that is often gray or black. Its original Greek name Haima means blood, and the Greeks were in love with it in the ancient world.[18] Hematite has been used throughout history, from a prehistoric etching tool to Native American war paint, and is even found in the tombs of Egyptian pharaohs. Wearing hematite will protect you from negativity, and keeping it in your home will help alleviate distractions for a more focused environment. This crystal cannot be cleansed with water, so try opting for smoke or other crystals instead.

Healing Properties

- Aids in blood-related disorders
- Helps with menstrual cycles
- Removes toxins from the body and mind
- Increases strength and vitality
- Protects against unwanted and harmful vibrations
- Enhances safety, security, and self-awareness through the root chakra

Labradorite

Labradorescence is the shimmering effect that we find in a labradorite crystal.[19] They often hold shades of blue, green, and gray and have tabular patterns throughout. For centuries, labradorite has been tied to the Aurora Borealis, and it has been found in Canada, Finland, and Russia. Wearing this crystal is good for harmony; inside the home, it can bring a calming water energy to the environment. Cleanse labradorite in water, but only briefly, as prolonged use can make it brittle. It also does great being cleansed and charged under the moonlight.

Healing Properties

- Helps with respiratory issues
- Enhances good digestion
- Wipes out anxiety
- Inspires our imagination to think in new ways
- Stabilizes our emotions and moods
- Links to the third eye chakra to connect to the spiritual realm

Lapis Lazuli

As a metamorphic rock, lapis lazuli is a mix of sodalite, pyrite, and calcite.[20] This crystal has diverse shades of blue and purple and has been used throughout the centuries for pigment and decorative jewelry. Also called the "wisdom stone" due to its connection to the third eye chakra, lapis lazuli has been adored throughout ancient cultures, including Egypt, Persia, and South America. Keeping this crystal in your home can prevent psychic attacks and enable positive communication. Lapis lazuli can be cleansed alongside other gemstones such as clear quartz, but refrain from using water as that can cause unwanted chemical reactions.

Healing Properties

- Alleviates insomnia and depression
- Connects to the throat chakra and heals the thyroid
- Reduces inflammation and repairs the nervous system
- Enhances self-awareness and fosters self-expression
- Inspires wisdom, intuition, and clarity

Lepidolite

Once called Lilalite, lepidolite is a lavender-colored gemstone that belongs to the mica group of minerals.[21] This crystal is found in places such as Brazil, California, Madagascar, and Russia. It is a soft stone, measuring 2.5 to 3.5 on the Mohs scale of hardness. Because of this, cleansing lepidolite requires a careful touch. This crystal will become brittle in water and may fade in color with prolonged exposure to sunlight, so using smoke to cleanse and charge it is ideal. Lepidolite is a balancing stone for the home, and wearing it in jewelry can provide protection.

Healing Properties

- Guards against EMFs
- Stabilizes moods and hormonal cycles
- Heals from within to support balanced emotions
- Corrects unwanted behavioral patterns
- Balances out the soul, body, and mind
- Completes the connection between the third eye, heart, and crown chakra

Malachite

Malachite is a seductively green gemstone that has been beloved by ancient Greeks and Egyptians alike.[22] It was even used as the pigment for Cleopatra's eye shadow. Today, malachite is found in the Amazon jungle and Egyptian mines. Keeping malachite in your home can help to prevent negative energy from coming inside. We can also wear malachites for heightened energy and additional protection. This crystal is a delicate one when it comes to cleansing and should be kept away from water to avoid chemical reactions. Do not leave it in the sunlight for more than a couple of hours, or it may fade, and avoid contact with salt because it can eat away at the smooth texture of the stone.

Healing Properties

- Heals the body quickly
- Aids in menstruation
- Minimizes and removes fears
- Clears away toxic emotions
- Enhances confidence and inner strength
- Allows us to accept change in a healthy way
- Clears blockages with the heart chakra

Moonstone

Moonstone is a feminine and dreamy stone that belongs to the feldspar mineral group.[23] It is available in many diverse colors, ones that are pale and often pearlescent. This gemstone has been included in witchcraft for centuries for its connection to the divine feminine nature of the universe. We can wear moonstones and jewelry to help us accept change, and when we place moonstones throughout our homes, it can clear away negative energy and allow room for a rebalancing of emotions. Moonstone can be cleansed with water, but not for extended periods, as that will cause physical damage to the stone. It also does well under the light of the moon.

Healing Properties

- Helps to balance the hormones
- Aid infertility
- Brings harmony during uncomfortable times
- Enhances psychic abilities
- Links to the third eye chakra
- Clears blockages in the crown chakra

Peridot

Peridot is a green gem that can come in all shades, from yellowish green to olive green, which is fitting since peridot is a form of olivine.[24] Legend has it that Cleopatra enjoyed peridot very much, as did other Egyptian queens, and some high priests of the ancient world would use this crystal to scare off evil spirits. Hailing from the Red Sea, the Greeks called this crystal Topazios, which is also the name of the island from where it is mined. Today we see peridots in Brazil, Hawaii, and Australia. Wearing peridot can help us raise our energy levels, and using it in the home can bring harmony and compassion to your environment. Peridot can be cleansed under moonlight or in the presence of vibrant plants, but it is a delicate stone and cannot handle abrasiveness or high temperatures.

Healing Properties

- Enables detoxification of the body
- Heals digestive problems
- Soothes muscle aches and contractions during labor
- Allows us to let go of jealousy and resentment
- Relieves anxiety and stress
- Focuses the mind and boosts energy for mental work
- Connects the solar plexus chakra and the heart chakra

Pyrite

Pyrite is also known as "Fool's Gold" due to its similarity with real gold.[25] This shiny metallic crystal is named after the Greek word for fire. It can be found throughout Spain, Mexico, Namibia, and Peru; throughout history, people used pyrite for protection. Wearing this crystal will bring not just protection but also increased energy. Because of its similarity to gold, pyrite can help to attract wealth to your home. This stone is a brittle one, so avoid submerging it in water, or it will rust. It is best when cleansed with smoke.

Healing Properties

- Stabilizes and brings strength to the wearer
- Increases stamina
- Wards off viral infections
- Helps with fertility and breathing troubles
- Increases confidence and reduces anxiety
- Removes blockages in both the solar plexus and sacral chakras
- Protects against EMFs

Red Garnet

Garnet has been in use for centuries, and most notably, it is said to have been the single source of light on Noah's ark.[26] Garnet is also seen in ancient Greek mythology, being tied to Persephone and the legend of her eating pomegranate seeds in the presence of Hades. This crystal is found in Sri Lanka, Madagascar, and India, and its deep reddish-purple tones link it directly to the root and solar plexus chakras. Jewelry that contains garnet has been discovered dating as far back as 3000 BC. Wearing garnet can provide raw and vibrant energy. When cleansing this stone, you can use soapy water and a simple rinse. You can also cleanse garnet around other crystals, such as clear quartz, but you will not want to use extended amounts of sunlight for cleansing as that can fade the garnet.

Healing Properties

- Increases self-confidence
- Creates sincerity
- Enhances sexual energy
- Removes toxins and stimulates circulation
- Grounds the mental body
- Provides security and feelings of safety

Red Jasper

Red Jasper is one version of the various colors of jasper that all have their unique abilities.[27] For red jasper, we can find protection, grounding effects, and vital passion. With this crystal, we can create courage and stamina while simultaneously raising our endurance for the day that lies ahead. This crystal is popular amongst ancient scholars and magicians, being used as a talisman for all sorts of strengthening purposes. Wearing red jasper will bring you protection, and when we place it in the home, especially the bedroom, it enhances pleasure. This crystal can be cleansed under the light of the moon, and it can also be rinsed off, but do not submerge it in water for too long, or it may rust.

Healing Properties

- Helps with circulation

- Balances out sexual energy
- Connects us to the physical world, so we remain mindful and present
- Sharpens our focus
- Is connected to the lower chakras

Rhodonite

Rhodonite is an opaque crystal that is often pink to red in color and has a triclinic crystal pattern.[28] The name of this crystal originates from the Greek word for rose and is found across the globe in places like Sweden, Australia, and India. Wear rhodonite in jewelry to help you recover from heartache as you heal from your feelings in a peaceful way. Keep rhodonite in your home to create balance and harmony within relationships. Cleanse this stone with a little bit of water and a soft towel, but do not submerge it in water for too long, or it can damage the crystal.

Healing Properties

- Invigorates new energy
- Connects to the heart chakra
- Aids in digestion
- Helps with autoimmune diseases and skin problems
- Inspires healing for the skin to prevent scarring

- Removes emotional wounds
- Allows for self-love to flourish

Rose Quartz

Rose quartz is a beautifully pale pink stone that has been in use for hundreds of years.[29] It holds the promise of compassion and love, not just for external relationships but also for self-love and self-esteem. This gemstone comes from places like Madagascar, Brazil, Japan, and the United States. It has been connected to both Adonis and Aphrodite, and throughout ancient civilizations, this crystal has played a pivotal role in healing practices. We can use rose quartz in the home to enhance the way we see ourselves in terms of beauty and self-esteem, and keeping a large crystal on display will help to enhance the environment with the positive, welcoming energy of love. Cleansing rose quartz can be done with moonlight or near candles, but do not leave it in the sun for more than a couple of hours, or it will fade.

Healing Properties

- Improves circulation and enhances the health of the heart
- Assists in a healthy and protected pregnancy
- Heals past emotional wounds and traumas

- Welcomes kindness and compassion
- Connects to the goddess and divine power

Selenite

Selenite is a delicate gemstone that comes from the gypsum mineral.[30] This stone is also called the "goddess stone." It can be pearlescent, opaque, and even milky white. Selenite is found in places like Japan, Argentina, and Greece, and it is the symbolic crystal of the ancient Greek moon goddess Selene. We can wear selenite to raise our vibrations and connect with the spirit realm. When placed within the home, this crystal can harmonize the environment with a blanket of white light. Selenite can be cleansed amongst other crystals, such as clear quartz. This delicate crystal should not be placed in water, even for a brief moment, because it is soft and can break away with even the smallest amount of exposure. Selenite can be cleansed with sunlight but shouldn't be exposed for more than a few hours as it can fade.

Healing Properties

- Connects to the crown chakra to clear away negativity
- Bridges the angelic realm with the physical realm

- Improves the skeletal system
- Reverses free radicals within the cells to keep you looking younger
- Clarifies issues that would otherwise cause confusion
- Removes worrisome thoughts and anxiety

Smoky Quartz

As a dusty brown variety of quartz, smoky quartz has a hexagonal crystal pattern and is anywhere from transparent to opaque.[31] This crystal is found in various parts of the world but is concentrated in Brazil. Smoky quartz is the national stone of Scotland, which they call Morion. The Celts found smoky quartz deep in the Cairngorm Mountains and used it for their clothing. Using smoky quartz in jewelry can help protect against negative energy, and keeping it in your home can protect your personal space from EMFs while also stimulating emotional grounding. You can cleanse this crystal with a quick wash, but do not leave it in the sun for cleansing, as that will cause it to fade.

Healing Properties

- Absorbs EMFs and helps to protect empaths
- Settles nerves and removes anxiety
- Detoxifies the body physically and emotionally

- Heals the emotions that leave us feeling distant and disconnected
- Links to the root chakra to keep us grounded and safe
- Aligns the base chakras

Sodalite

Sodalite is a richly blue-colored stone with pockets of white, and it contains the cubic crystal pattern with a luster that is described as waxy.[32] Having been discovered during the 19th century, sodalite was found in Greenland and Canada near icy winds and snowcapped mountains. We can wear sodalite to bring positive thoughts and peacefulness after stressful moments. Keeping this crystal in your home or office can enhance your self-worth. Sodalite can be cleansed under running water, but don't submerge it, or it will break. It can also be cleansed by moonlight, but using sunlight can cause it to fade.

Healing Properties

- Connects to the throat chakra to help with head colds and throat discomfort
- Boosts the immune system and reduces fevers
- Enhances graceful communication
- Inspires artists and writers alike

- Bridges the gap between abstract thoughts and the tangible Earth
- Enables us to be truthful to ourselves while open to new possibilities

Tiger's Eye

Tiger's eye is a brilliant bronze gemstone with a silkiness to its appearance.[33] It is among the many types of metamorphic rocks that belong to the chalcedony mineral group. This crystal has long been used to protect against curses, and it is found in places like South Africa, India, and Australia. Tiger's eye was also a beloved gem for the ancient Egyptians, and it was placed on the breastplates of Roman soldiers. Tiger's eye is great for personal protection and can be added to jewelry for this reason. You can also place a Tiger's eye specimen in the home to create a blanket of balance. Avoid exposing raw Tiger's eye to water because it can be toxic.

Healing Properties

- Raises energy to remove lethargy
- Boosts metabolism to a healthy level
- Wipes away negative energy
- Increases self-worth and confidence
- Provides secure and safe feelings

- Clears blockages in the root chakra
- Heightens psychic abilities

Turquoise

Turquoise is a bold bluish-green stone that resembles the ocean. Hailing from places like Nova Scotia, Namibia, Tibet, and the Mojave Desert, turquoise is a sacred stone to many native tribes across the globe.[34] Some of the older specimens date back to 6000 BC around the Sinai Peninsula in Egypt. The Navajo and Zuni cultures have long been creating jewelry and talismans made with turquoise to help heal and cleanse. For this reason, turquoise makes a great addition to any piece of jewelry. Turquoise can be placed in your home to bring soothing water energy into the environment. Turquoise does well with smoke cleansing but should avoid water because it may be subject to chemical reactions, fading, and cracking. We also shouldn't leave turquoise under the sunlight for too long because it can cause the brilliant colors to fade.

Healing Properties

- Heals and opens the throat chakra
- Helps with allergies, respiratory problems, and migraines
- Calms emotions and provides serenity

- Enhances compassionate communication
- Inspires spiritual transformation

KEEP HEADING TOWARD RELIEF

Now that we have an idea of which crystals are most necessary in a beginner's tool kit, we can focus on the true healing of each crystal. Let's head into the next chapter, where we will address specific troubles and how crystals can help to heal each one.

6

QUICK START REFERENCE GUIDE FOR DIFFERENT AILMENTS

With your new knowledge of how to cleanse and program your stones and the main stones that are best for a beginner's collection, we can now take a look at what each stone can be used for in regards to healing and helping to improve our lives. Each crystal has different applications, so throughout this chapter, you may see several of them mentioned more than once. This is just a testament to nature's fantastic abilities and how certain vibrations can impact different parts of the body and mind.

Throughout this chapter, you will also find recommendations for certain crystals depending on the ailment of focus. This simple guide will help kickstart your journey, but if you feel drawn to a different type of crystal, try it out and see how it works for you. Part of being an intuitive witch is learning to feel the energy around you and knowing when to act. Our deeper consciousness is capable of picking up exactly what we need for our lives. If we trust it and pay attention to our feelings as we approach crystals, then we will be able to select the right one for us. And sometimes, the right one isn't always the obvious one.

Let's keep an open mind as we address the common ailments people like to treat with crystals. This is a typical list that will help you begin practicing healing with your crystals as you get to know them even better than before. Remember that you should always work with crystals you have already cleansed, bonded with, and programmed to align with your energy. That way, you are both in sync with what you are trying to manifest.

ALLEVIATING DEPRESSION AND SADNESS

Carnelian, Citrine, Lepidolite, Tiger's Eye

Depression affects everyone at various points in their lives, and it can be difficult to pull ourselves out of situations where we feel overly sad. Sometimes this can be due to our energy being depleted, or it might be because we are focused on the things that are only causing us harm or grief. By using crystals to remove the sad energy from our bodies, we can move past our depression a little easier than if we were to wait it out. Also, using crystals along with western medicine can help to repair the flow of energy so that you may not need to rely on medications long-term.

PROMOTING AND SUSTAINING HAPPINESS

Citrine, Rose Quartz, Peridot, Clear Quartz, Tiger's Eye

Along with relieving our depression and sadness, we can focus on promoting happiness to help ourselves overcome what is bothering us. Typically, crystals that are brightly colored can help to bring warmth and sunshine quality to our lives. Also, the ones that help increase love and sympathy are great at boosting our happiness levels. At times we may need some help with sustaining happiness, especially since, in our busy lives, so many factors come into play and can cause our days to go in different directions than we had planned.

HANDLING FRUSTRATION AND ANGER

Amethyst, Rose Quartz, Peridot, Smoky Quartz

Frustration is a natural emotion that many of us experience on a daily basis. This can be due to a build-up of negative energy that is holding us back from forgiving and forgetting. These crystals can help us process the anger we are dealing with in a healthy way, allowing the energy to flow through us freely and move on out of our bodies. Through this process, the frustration turns into acceptance and forgiveness. When we use crystals to resolve this energy blockage, we not only feel better physically, but our mental state can resolve the problems that are keeping us angry.

EASING ANXIETY AND STRESS

Amethyst, Rose Quartz, Black Tourmaline, Lepidolite, Blue Lace Agate, Sodalite

Our modern lives are full of stressful incidents. Even minor setbacks in our daily routines can cause us stress, but when we deal with more challenging issues, we face excessive pressure that can lead to anxiety. Our natural bodies are capable of withstanding a lot, both physically and mentally, and it is in our nature to try and resolve our problems ourselves so that we remain strong and virile. But because we do this by bottling up anxiety and stress, our bodies take a toll, and we end up feeling jittery and strung out. Suppose we allow ourselves to dive too deep into our thoughts. In that case, we can sometimes get lost in the what-ifs, which ends up over-whelming our bodies with excessive amounts of energy. Instead of overworking our minds and body, we can call on the power of crystals to help increase the energy flow throughout our energy centers. This causes the stress to melt away and become a tiny obstacle that is easier to overcome. Sometimes it takes a little retrospect to realize that the things we are stressing over are not typically as weighty as we make them out to be, which is truly a case of mind over matter.

IMPROVING SLEEP

Amethyst, Rose Quartz, Selenite, Lepidolite, Moonstone, Black Tourmaline, Angelite

Along with all of these other issues that we deal with because of our modern and chaotic lives, trying to get enough sleep is one of the top priorities that we often let slide. Having enough sleep can allow our bodies to deal with stressful situations a little bit easier, which means that we can handle the negative energy that comes our way and process it in a healthy way to resolve it. It all starts with a proper diet and plenty of sleep. Using crystals to help you fall asleep and have a restful night is the first way you can alleviate issues like depression, anxiety, and anger. Some of these crystals, such as amethyst, are great at facilitating dreams that nurture our souls just as much as our bodies.

DIMINISHING HEADACHES AND MIGRAINES

Rose Quartz, Amethyst, Clear Quartz, Selenite, Lapis Lazuli

It's no secret that people suffering from the aforementioned troubles often end up with headaches and migraines. These can be debilitating for people who cannot avoid their daily routines, such as getting the kids off to school or making it to work through the morning commute. The added noise and visual stimulation only make headaches and migraines worse. As I said before, addressing the root problems of stress and not getting enough sleep will help to alleviate headaches and migraines before they begin. But if you're in the moment and a headache comes on, then using one of these crystals can drastically change how you feel. Allow the soothing energy flow of a cleansed and programmed crystal such as selenite to remove the blockage and intensity of the headache you are experiencing.

You can view a headache as a buildup of energy quite easily because it is as though all the emotions and the physical stresses you are dealing with bottle up and have nowhere to go. Part of this is because we aren't processing our stress in a healthy way. Instead, allow crystals to help reduce pressure as the energy within your body begins to flow more naturally. It's all about allowing your thoughts to accept the way things are so that you can process what is troubling you in a healthy way and resolve those feelings and emotions.

ASSISTING IN FERTILITY, PREGNANCY, AND BIRTH

Rose Quartz, Amethyst, Moonstone, Carnelian

Some of us spend a good portion of our young adult lives thinking about and trying to become pregnant. To aid in fertility and a more pleasant pregnancy, use crystals to help the energy in and around you become aligned with your intentions of having a child. A lot is involved when becoming pregnant, such as blood circulation, and some crystals can help keep this type of energy flowing in a healthy way. Some women who do not have difficulty becoming pregnant or carrying their children might still find themselves worried or stressed over the labor. Every woman's body is different from the next, and no two cases of labor will ever be quite the same. Preparing for this big event by aligning your chakras and bringing your energy to its best state possible will help ease your mind and possibly even the physical experience altogether.

CASTING ENERGETIC PROTECTION

Black Tourmaline, Amethyst, Black Obsidian, Clear Quartz

No matter what it is we are doing in our lives, we often feel as though we need protection from outside influences. This is where crystals can truly shine, in that they can offer us protection against other energy sources around us. Even something simple like grocery shopping can leave us vulnerable to absorbing energy from the people around us and the building itself. Of course, there's also residual energy left on objects throughout the store from hundreds of people passing through regularly. When we arm ourselves with protection from these excessive amounts of variable energy, we can keep our routine trips positive and beneficial.

Of course, our daily routines are not the only area where we need protection. Sometimes we want to protect ourselves from natural disasters, car accidents, or other unfortunate events. We might want to protect our families when we travel to new places. During cold and flu season, we may want to protect ourselves by boosting our immunities and keeping the sickness at bay. There are truly thousands of different opportunities where we can protect both our physical and mental bodies and those of the people we love and care about. Crystals can serve many purposes regarding protection, whether it be warding off energy or blocking harmful influences altogether.

MANIFESTING LOVE

Rose Quartz, Malachite, Green Aventurine, Moonstone

We all crave a sense of love and belonging. Sometimes it's a matter of opening our minds and our energies to the possibility of a new person or a new flame. Sometimes we overlook the people who are already making an impact in our lives, and in these situations, crystals can help us see the good that is before us. We can manifest love and romance and kindle new friendships by using crystals. Certain crystals will nurture compassion and kindness and allow us to find true love hidden deep within solid friendships. Other crystals can help us learn to love ourselves and to accept who we are, as we are, and to resolve the anxieties and sadness that we carry around for our self-image.

Creating romance through crystals can provide us with a pure and wholehearted intimate relationship that fulfills our physical and mental desires. When we are looking for that connection to help us feel as though we belong and that we have a place in this world, it often comes not only from physical attraction but also from deep within the heart. Our minds connect, just as our souls will, and we create lasting partnerships with the people who can truly benefit us in our lives.

CREATING WEALTH, ABUNDANCE, AND PROSPERITY

Citrine, Aventurine, Pyrite, Jade, Clear Quartz

Crystals are fantastic at creating wealth and abundance, and by using them in our meditations and during spell work and rituals, we can manifest prosperity and a better life. Sometimes it's a matter of providing the crystal with a purpose to seek out new opportunities and help us fulfill our dreams of financial freedom. Everyone wants to be independent and to be able to afford a comfortable lifestyle where they are healthy and happy. With crystals, we can pour our energy into this intention to make a fundamental change in our lives.

BUILDING GOOD HEALTH

Amethyst, Citrine, Lapis Lazuli, Rose Quartz

Perhaps one of the most common reasons people turn to crystals is to help heal the body and the mind. Crystals hold immense amounts of healing energy bestowed upon them by Mother Nature herself. Everything in nature is cyclical in how it will be born, grow, and then pass on. This endless cycle feeds into the next generation as we all continue to flourish together as one big and harmonious collective soul. Asking nature for her help to replenish your energy so we can relieve blockages and remove illnesses is exactly what we are meant to do. Our organic bodies and timeless souls are all a part of this woven fabric of consciousness that we call energy. Through it, we can influence the negative energies that are holding us back and causing us pain, and we can resolve them and transform them into good. And this is how healing begins.

ENCOURAGING CREATIVITY AND INSPIRATION

Carnelian, Citrine, Tiger's Eye, Lapis Lazuli, Garnet

Our ability to be creative and inspire change and progression is at the heart of our humanity. Many of us walk the earth seeking out new creativity, while some are also deeply involved in creative fields of work. It is our passions and hobbies that drive us to think of the world in a way that it could be rather than how it currently is. This creativity brings forth a new sense of novelty; because of that, we can transcend what is currently holding us back. Creative minds discover problems that are detrimental to society as a whole, and they work tirelessly to implement something new to help people overcome their struggles. Crystals can help people open their eyes to new possibilities and new outcomes so that the troubles of today become something of the past, moving humanity forward to continue to progress into a better life.

ENHANCING FOCUS, MOTIVATION, AND PRODUCTIVITY

Clear Quartz, Tiger's Eye, Smoky Quartz, Aventurine, Fluorite

Motivation and focus go hand in hand with creativity and prosperity. To become motivated, we must find a source of inspiration. In the same respect, we must first remain diligent and focused to find wealth and success. Using crystals to align with these three types of energies will help to create a system that can drive you deep into your passions for a prosperous outcome. Some crystals for motivation are aimed at helping us focus mentally on what we are spending our time on and how we continue to place our thoughts and intentions into our work. Other crystals may help us be physically motivated to accomplish things that might seem difficult or overwhelming. In either case, crystals are excellent at keeping our minds set on the goal at hand and amping up our desire to get up and seize the day.

CREATING NEW BEGINNINGS

Amazonite, Citrine, Moonstone, Kyanite, Labradorite

Throughout life, we may face issues that we'd like to just step away from for a while, if not permanently. This may involve relationships, careers, or even living situations. Whatever the case, there are a plethora of crystals that can assist in manifesting opportunities for new beginnings. Sometimes our choices are right before us, but we are too blinded by the current troubles weighing our minds. In a sea of uncertainty, crystals can help guide us in the right direction by helping us see what we cannot.

BOOSTING COURAGE AND CONFIDENCE

Carnelian, Tiger's Eye, Amazonite

Along with new beginnings and claiming the success that we wish for ourselves, we must allow ourselves to embrace our inner confidence. A low sense of self can take away our courage and leave us feeling inadequate. Before long, we feel the strains of stress and depression. Take back your confidence and boost your courage with the use of intensely rich-colored gemstones and crystals. Ones that are golden or orange can spark creativity for our self-image and help manifest the bravery you need to go out and make your mark on the world.

RELIEVING PAIN THROUGH ENERGY CENTERS

When we talk about relieving pain for our physical, mental, and spiritual bodies, we can directly address the chakra responsible for that energy center. For example, when we want to alleviate joint pain in our knees, we will want to focus on the root chakra as that is the one associated with the lower extremities. Referring to the different body parts and the mental ailments that can occur because of blockages, each chakra has its own associated areas of the body. To work on these areas, we can use the following crystals and place them onto the chakras on our bodies, as described in Chapter Three.

Root Chakra: Black Tourmaline
Sacral Chakra: Carnelian
Solar Plexus Chakra: Citrine
Heart Chakra: Rose Quartz
Throat Chakra: Aquamarine
Third Eye Chakra: Lapis Lazuli
Crown Chakra: Amethyst

STEPPING UP THE CRYSTAL'S POWER

Now that we've covered the basics of crystal healing, we can take a deeper look at how to harness the power of your chosen crystals. Crystals don't just help with our bodies; they also have powerful vibrations that can impact the environment around us. Learning how to utilize crystals in all aspects of your daily life will help to bring forth the intentions that you've set. Let's head into the next chapter as we talk more about allowing crystals to flourish in your home, office, and even your car. When we find a beautiful crystal specimen, we don't simply want to use it hidden away during solitary meditation. We want to keep it on display so it can continue to emit positive energy all day long.

7

HARNESSING THE POWER OF YOUR CRYSTALS

*C*rystals are not just about healing our energy centers; and they have many more uses than simply being used for meditation. With crystals, we can enhance our entire lives, whether at home, at work, or while we are out driving or being active. We can take crystals with us anywhere we go, and their healing energy and guiding light can help us in any situation we can think of. There are countless varieties of crystals across the globe, each with its own plethora of different abilities. Because of this, we can find one that suits our current desires and some that reveal themselves to us, letting us know that there are things we need to work on even when we aren't aware.

Certain crystals are great at protecting and keeping negative energies at bay, while others can invoke an atmosphere of love and compassion. Referring back to Chapter Five, we can choose specific crystals for our intentions and then place them around our homes, offices, and even in our cars to keep the positive energy and high vibrations flowing.

CRYSTAL USES THROUGHOUT HISTORY

Even though we have no written record of exactly when we began using crystals and stones as a human species, we can say that we've always been fascinated by the magic they hold. Going back to the upper pale-olithic, which was over 60,000 years ago, beads of natural elements like mammoth ivory and fossilized shark teeth have been discovered.[1] These are only some examples of the vast number of talismans and amulets that have been discovered across the globe.

According to scientists, some of the oldest amulets are made from Baltic amber, dating nearly 30,000 years ago. Aside from being used in jewelry, crystals have been a part of ritualistic ceremonies for just as long. For the ancient Sumerians, crystals were used to create magical formulas, and the ancient Egyptians also used various crystals found in that region for their jewelry. Looking further into civilization, the ancient Greeks would use certain crystals because they believed they held various properties. For the Chinese, jade is and has always been highly valued, and even around 1000 years ago, some Chinese emperors wore jade armor when buried. In all this time, these crystals were valued for healing, protecting, and granting wishes so that people could live better, more prosperous lives.

Although the Christian Church banned the use of amulets in 355AD, the belief held by many different types of people and cultures prevailed. Before long, even the Bishop of Rennes during the 11th century made the bold statement that wearing agate could make a person more agreeable to God. Furthermore, crystals have almost always been part of many diverse religions, including Hinduism, Buddhism, Islam, and Judaism. For example, the breastplate of Aaron, also called the "High Priest's Breastplate" from the book of Exodus in the Bible, is the basis for modern-day birthstones. Also, the fourth heaven listed in the Koran is said to be entirely composed of garnet. In Hinduism, the Kalpa Tree is said to be made of precious stone, and the throne near the Tree of Knowledge in Buddhism is made from diamonds.

As we continue through history, we can see that crystals are not only tied to spirituality but also have properties and abilities rooted in science. Just as we discussed in Chapter Two, we may not always have understood the science behind energy healing, which could also be said for other properties of gemstones and crystals. During the Renaissance, European people relied on crystals to treat certain diseases and illnesses. Used in conjunction with herbal medicine, many practitioners wholeheartedly believed in the ability of crystals to resolve problems that humanity had yet to truly understand.

Certain cultures, such as Native Americans, Aborigines, and Maoris, have never turned their backs on nature. These people, who are typically tribal-based and grounded in their spirituality, revere certain crystals as sacred. Still, to this day, these people continue with their spiritual practice as they focus on keeping harmony with nature.

Though we may have strayed from crystal healing in our western-minded world, the crystals have not lost any of their potency. While we continue to move toward a new collective age, both spiritually and physically, humankind has undoubtedly begun to desire a more simple and meaningful life. We've come so far in terms of technology and advancements, but we cannot ignore the desire to turn back and connect with nature as we once did millennia ago. These thoughts brought forth the new age culture during the 1900s, and once people started to see how beautiful their lives could become through the use of crystals, there was no turning back.

MAINTAINING AN ENERGETIC BOND WITH YOUR CRYSTALS

We've now gone through the journey of selecting the right crystal for ourselves, cleansing it, and programming it with our intentions. After going through this process, we want to address how to keep this crystal close so we can continue benefiting from its abilities. Crystals can radiate vibrations and send their energy to nearby sources, such as our bodies and places within our house, so we want to be near these crystals to enjoy what they have to offer. After all the work you've done to make that crystal your own, the last thing you want to do is tuck it in a drawer and forget about it. Avoiding the latter will enhance your intentions and further connect them with reality, helping you heal and grow in the ways that you seek.

Just like how we can recharge our crystals under the light of the moon, we can recharge our bodies by connecting with these crystals on a regular basis. This involves either carrying the crystal around with you in your pocket or handbag or placing the crystal in parts of your home or car, for example, to allow the healing energy to billow out around you.

Anytime we feel drained or need the support of our crystals, we can easily pick one up and have a quick meditation to feel the energy within us replenish. Some crystals are associated with different deities. If you've chosen a spiritual path with your crystals, you may want to communicate with those deities while holding the crystal for amplified power. Likewise, you might have a spirit guide, perhaps someone who has passed on that you knew very well, and you may want to communicate with that person. Using crystals to connect so that you can find guidance and answers to what is troubling you is a perfect way to utilize the power of nature in our everyday lives. This cannot happen if the crystals are tucked away and forgotten about.

An easy way to reconnect with and use our crystals daily is through meditation, which can take as little as five minutes. You may want to spend longer working with your crystals to further enhance the bond you are developing. This may also help to resolve the issues you're having with your energy centers.

Let's go through a few quick meditation ideas that you can use as a basis for your own practice to strengthen your bond with your crystals.

MEDITATING WITH YOUR CRYSTALS

With this meditation, we are not working on programming our crystals as we had before. Instead, we are allowing our physical bodies to absorb the energy of the crystal for healing and other purposes.[2] This is a time when we will give ourselves up to the energy and magic of the crystal and, in doing so, allow our mental and spiritual selves to heal on a much higher level than we could with meditation alone.

One simple way to meditate with your crystal is to hold it in your hand during your normal meditation practice. With this type of meditation, we sit with our eyes closed as we hold on to the crystal and allow the energy to seep into our fingertips and our palms until it begins to radiate throughout our bodies. This will feel similar to when you programmed your crystal, except the energy will be in reverse this time.

Another way to use crystals during meditation is by placing them directly onto the chakra you are focusing on. As we reviewed in Chapter Three, each chakra is an energy center that directly correlates to certain ailments and difficulties experienced throughout the physical and mental body. To fix these problems and free the flow of energy, we can use a crystal to stimulate healing. We place the crystal directly onto the energy center and allow it to radiate throughout that region of our body.

Another great meditation technique is to use crystals associated with the third eye chakra and to spend time allowing their energies to fill you and open your psychic abilities. Connecting with your psychic self will allow you to be more intuitive and open to things that our physical bodies have difficulty seeing. This will enable you to connect with the crystals on a deeper level as your cosmic energies become more aligned and attuned to one another.

Aside from meditation, we can bring crystals into our living spaces to continue the positive energy flow. Crystals can do many wonderful things, but most importantly, they allow us to find that power deep within and unleash our capabilities. This gives crystal witches untold amounts of energy and power.

DECORATING WITH YOUR CRYSTALS

A very powerful way to continue your crystal work as you go about your day is to incorporate crystals throughout your environment.[3] Placing them throughout your home, your office, and even in your car can help bring the energies into your life in a continuous and plentiful way. Let's look at the various places we can add our crystals and some starter suggestions for types of crystals that do best in those environments.

Bedroom

Rose Quartz, Amethyst, Selenite

The bedroom is a sanctuary for us to relax and rejuvenate. It is where we rest and attempt to find calmness in our hectic routines. Placing crystals such as rose quartz, amethyst, and selenite will allow your physical body to find the piece that it is after. At the same time, these crystals also work to help provide us with good dreams, and, in the case of amethyst, we are also working at opening our third eye chakra to enhance our psychic abilities.

Bathroom

Clear Quartz, Rose Quartz

Your bathroom is another place in your home where we look for rest. Through our personal care routines, including hygiene and feel-good personal grooming practices, the bathroom enables us to replenish from the inside out. Because of this, clear quartz and rose quartz are exceptional at helping keep the flow of energy at the right vibration for the bathroom.

Living Room

Amethyst, Fluorite

The living room can often be a high-traffic zone with lots of energy and diverse emotions. It is a place where we gather and communicate and is meant to be cozy and comfortable. Because of this mix of vibrations, it's good to have crystals such as amethyst and fluorite on display. Amethyst is exceptional at keeping the energies of the environment balanced and pure, and fluorite can help in social gatherings to allow for healthy self-expression and wholesome communication.

Kitchen

Citrine, Carnelian

Our kitchens are a place of inspiration and creativity. It is where we come together and enjoy each other's presence as we feast on nature's bounty. Oftentimes, the kitchen is also a place for us to relax and process the day's events. For this reason, we can use crystals such as citrine and carnelian to keep the energy of the room light and sunny. These crystals not only invoke courage and compassion, but they also bring warmth to a much-admired family room.

Front Door

Black Tourmaline

The front door of our homes is highly important when it comes to warding off energies that we do not want to be involved in our lives. To prevent people from bringing their negativity into your home, using a crystal, like black tourmaline, is the perfect way to ward off these energies. Black tourmaline also absorbs negativity, so it isn't just preventing those energies from entering your home; it is expelling them completely. Before any guests arrive, place the black tourmaline on your entry table or even add it to the wreath that is hanging on your front door.

Office

Tiger's Eye, Pyrite, Black Tourmaline

Your work office, especially in a highly public place where many people come and go, can be full of various types of energy. To remain focused throughout the workday, keep black tourmaline on display on your desk. In addition, pyrite is a great crystal to help amplify prosperity so that you can be successful in the work you do. And finally, using tiger's eye in your office can boost your confidence and creativity while simultaneously warding off negativity.

Vehicle

Black Obsidian, Clear Quartz, Tiger's Eye

As far as your vehicle goes, keeping crystals either on display or positioned throughout will help you stay protected and focused while driving. In addition, some crystals can even help you with handling car sickness. Using black obsidian, tiger's eye, and clear quartz in your car will help make the ride more comfortable and safe.

WALKING DEEPER INTO YOUR CRYSTAL PATH

Now that we've been through all these different places where we can keep our crystals, we can move forward and talk about how to facilitate a crystal healing spell. This is one of the fun things that crystal witches get to do in their practice. Aside from meditation and using crystals in our environments, a crystal spell is exceptional at driving home the pure energy needed to resolve the illnesses or diseases that are ailing you. So let's head into the next chapter, where we examine how to perform a crystal healing spell.

8

5 EASY STEPS TO PERFORM A CRYSTAL HEALING SPELL

*P*erforming a crystal healing spell is like taking your healing to the next level. When we use spells, we are directly invoking the energies around us and willing them to bring our intentions to light. This is also considered a form of manifestation, in which we have a desire that we need to accomplish, and we put every bit of our energy into seeing it come to life.

We can think of a spell as a way to speak directly with the energies surrounding us and ask them to perform the actions we need to be done on a metaphysical level. For example, we say the words out loud for the spell to set forth our intentions for the energy to heal a specific area of the body. While we do this, we are also using energy from the rest of our physical bodies to brighten and overflow the area that needs help. This amplified energy boost is the metaphysical basis of a spell, and all types of witches use it differently.

The way we use crystals during a spell is by enlisting our own energy and the energy of the crystal to raise the body's vibrations. In doing this, we connect with the healing energy flow of the crystal on both a meta-physical and tangible level. During a spell, we not only believe that the energy has risen and brightened around us, but we can feel it in our fingertips and throughout our bones. This is the beauty of magic; it is exactly how we work with energy during a spell to use crystals to heal in amplified ways.

TAKE YOUR TIME TO GROW WITH YOUR MAGIC

All the information in this book can be overwhelming, especially for people who are new to a magical lifestyle. With magic, and especially when we speak of the meta-physical and tangible world coming together throughout nature, there are countless connections to account for. Each plant has a connection to each energy center within us. So too, do the trees, the animals, and the celestial bodies in the heavens above us. It is the same for crystals.

With all the different ways that crystals can help us, it might be confusing where to start. This is especially true when speaking about spells and rituals because they can sometimes involve extra steps and more ingredients than a beginner expects. Whether you're a seasoned witch or someone who is just starting out, there may be times when things don't quite make sense, and you feel that there is just too much going on around you to grasp it all. Despite this, you must remember that this is all part of your journey and your growth as a witch.

No one has ever set out on this adventure without making a few mistakes along the way. We are human, and thus we are not perfect, but this is the way nature designed us. We are perfectly imperfect, make mistakes, and mess up when we least expect it, which is all part of the learning process we must go through to find our true selves and reveal our power deep within. We cannot step into a magical or healing life full of crystals with all the answers. We begin with a good understanding of what we need and how we can go about resolving the problems that are ailing us, but from there, it is up to us to learn and grow.

Do not worry about understanding everything from the very beginning. Successful and prosperous witches often have one thing in common: their ability to keep an open mind about how they can continue to improve with their practices. Let this journey take hold as you embrace this new pass and allow the magic of nature to filter into your life. This is how we gain experience in our practice, and it is exactly how you build your intuition. The only way to embark on this journey is to take the first step and get into the metaphysical and magical world that has intrigued you for so long.

THE TRUE MEANING AND VALUE OF CRYSTAL SPELLS

Spellwork can help further your bond with your crystals. Among the many benefits, they offer a nice way for you to relax your mind while following the simple, orderly methods described. Because rituals can be very orderly, organized by step-by-step processes that tell you exactly what to do and how to do it, you can take the guesswork out of your magic and allow it to just be. Removing our thoughts and emotions from the practice lets us truly become one with our crystals. We are free from the negative thoughts that bother us, and we can focus on our intentions and the good we wish to create for ourselves. This can detach us from our worrisome thoughts and allow our bodies to truly become aligned with the energy of the crystal.

If you find extra time to devote to your crystal, I highly recommend learning this framework, understanding its meaning, and trying it out for yourself. Eventually, you'll be able to branch out and integrate it into your own personal practice with your unique twists and contributions. Committing to this will truly enhance the way you feel and work with your chosen crystals. And this is exactly why spellwork is so effective. We can let go of everything else, the worry, the pain, the fear, and simply focus on the spell and its purpose. This is the root of empowerment and the most important part of becoming a strong crystal witch. When you can release the things that are holding you down, things that have no business occupying your precious thoughts, then you can sharpen your focus on your true intentions and manifest the life you so desire.

THE SIMPLE FIVE-STEP FRAMEWORK FOR CRYSTAL SPELLS

Before performing your first crystal healing spell, we will go through this five-step framework that you can apply to all your future healing spells. This framework simplifies the spell itself while providing a bit of wiggle room for you to customize future spells to your liking. Throughout these steps, remember that this is simply a culmination of everything discussed and learned throughout this book so far. If there's information that you need to review, you can pause and revert back to the previous chapter to find more details and answers to your questions.

1. Identify What You Are Seeking with Crystal Empowerment

Your first step in creating a crystal healing spell is to identify what it is you are trying to resolve or enhance. Are you trying to alleviate pain or discomfort? Are you hoping to resolve the anxiety that you have during certain activities? Asking yourself the deepest questions at this first stage will guide you into creating a spell that will cater exactly to the troubles you're experiencing.

This step is crucial to the overall spell because it will set forth your initial intentions. As we spoke about in Chapter Two, your intentions are highly powerful and influence the energy you manipulate through the use of crystals. Having clear intentions will enable you to resolve your troubles quicker and easier than if you are uncertain about your goals.

Remember that your intentions are also affected by your emotions and feelings. For us to align our energy centers with positive energy, we must be focused and clear on what it is we are trying to manifest. Uncertainty can cause our thoughts to stray and become tainted with toxicity and fear. Before beginning the spell itself, you should ask yourself as many questions as possible to fully understand what you are hoping to achieve.

2. Choose a Crystal to Align with Your Goal

The second step in our healing spell framework is choosing a crystal that will help resolve your troubles. Remember that each crystal has properties of its own, and because of those properties, the crystal can heal in different ways. Many crystals have multiple abilities, such as protecting and keeping us grounded. Crystals can be about much more than simply healing, so finding the right one for your goal is vital to the overall spell.

We can use crystals to improve and align our energy centers simply because the crystal is the same color that is associated with the energy center. Additionally, we can use crystals to help us focus on a particular emotion or feeling so that we are able to heal from the inside out. Referring back to Chapter Six, we can pinpoint a specific type of ailment and find a crystal that correlates with resolving those difficulties. Crystals are capable of restoring the mind and the body to not only a state of contentment but also one that makes a person feel as though they are thriving.

In Chapter Five, we discussed thirty-four crystals that I recommend for all to begin their collections with. Going back to our list there, you can easily find good remedies for the many common problems we all face regularly.

3. Cleanse the Crystal Before Use

Before we can use our crystals for a healing spell, we must cleanse them properly. As discussed in Chapter Four, there are different methods for cleansing our crystals. Depending on your type of crystal, you can use the elements, natural items from the outdoors, and even your breath to cleanse your crystals before use.

Remember that this step is significant to your use of crystals because all crystals and gemstones will carry residual energy within them. These energies can sway your intentions and alter the outcome of your healing, whether it be through meditation, spells, or rituals. Energy comes from all sorts of places and people, and because crystals are the types of items we like to pick up and examine firsthand, everyone that has passed through the shop where you purchased your gemstone or crystal has left their mark on that item.

Cleansing our crystals allows us to build a more profound and robust connection with them. Not only are we removing other people's energy from the crystal, but we are also taking the time to reset it to its original state. This act alone creates a strong bond simply because we are taking the time to help the crystal become renewed.

4. Program Your Crystal with Your Intentions

From the original goal you had focused on in step one, we can now sharpen our intentions and program the crystal to perform what is needed for healing. Sometimes all it takes is to become more attuned to the energy within the crystal so that our bodies, both physically and mentally, are aligned with the right healing energy necessary to resolve what is troubling us.

Again, the act of simply spending time with our crystals as we pour our energy into them, along with our intentions, brings us a deeper connection to the crystal itself. The bonds we build between our energy and the crystal's energy become the structure of our energy work. We are further connecting our energy to a web of energy that is underneath everything we see in the physical world.

By using what we learned in Chapter Four, we can program our crystals so that our energies are linked and focused on our intentions. Mother Nature is fantastic at creating all of her bountiful objects, and each of them knows exactly what purpose it has in the world. Programming our crystals with our intentions is not about telling the crystal what it should and should not do. It is more about connecting with the energy of the right crystal and letting it know that it now has purpose in your life.

5. Decide on How to Channel the Crystal's Energy

With the previous four steps out of the way, it is now time to decide how we will channel the energy within the crystal. How would you like to harness this energy that you have helped nurture into the exact intentions you have named? How can you use this crystal to empower your healing and make you stronger and happier?

Throughout Chapter Seven, we discussed the various ways to use a crystal after it has been programmed. With the crystal fully cleansed and ready for use, there are many options for how to use it, wear it as jewelry, or place it in your home or office. Reviewing Chapter Seven will help you identify what is best for the crystal and for the intentions that you have set forth.

Sometimes it is as simple as carrying the crystal around in your pocket as you go about your day. Not only are you using it in one of the many ways to channel its energy and reap the benefits, but you are also continuing to build the bond you began during the cleansing stage of your crystal.

MAINTAINING THE CONNECTION AND GOOD VIBES

Once you complete this process, take the time to enjoy and bask in the presence of your crystal's positive vibes. Be grateful for the bond you have formed and the help it will provide as you seek out the answers and solutions to your desires. Remember that your crystals can surprise you and help you in different ways, even in ways you never expected. Your crystal now has everything it needs to guide and support you on your path. Although you have successfully cast a crystal spell, your journey and relationship with your crystal has just begun!

As mentioned before in Chapter Four, you may need to occasionally re-cleanse your crystal. What's recommended as a general rule of thumb is to cleanse at least once a month. You can tell if it needs cleansing sooner based on the weight and nature of the energy it is emitting. If you sense the feeling that you have lost the connection with your crystal, you can opt to reprogram it. This will reestablish the bond you created and realign your energies for that shared purpose. If you feel like you need an extra boost for the day, you can meditate with your crystal to amplify the bond, as explained in Chapter Seven. From there, you can continue strengthening this relationship as you go through your enlightenment journey, with your crystal guiding you every step of the way. Lastly, if you would ever like to cast another spell using the same crystal for different intentions, simply repeat the five-step framework again.

SAMPLE SPELLS TO HELP GET YOU STARTED

Remember that using crystals can have its ups and downs, especially when it comes to the detailed and often lengthy practice of casting spells. To ease this, I've included three of my spells that can give you an idea of how a crystal healing spell will play out. For each of these spells, it's important to know that the chosen crystal and method go hand in hand. Once you are more familiar with what crystals can do for your life, you can adjust these spells as a framework for the future spells that you want to craft on your own. Healing and protecting with crystals through crystal magic is a highly personal experience, and we can customize every aspect of this type of witchcraft to suit our needs.

Energy Protection Spell

This spell is intended to provide protection against negative energy so that you feel grounded in your environment rather than loose and aimless. This can provide feelings of safety and security as well since you will be able to discern the difference between your own energy and that of the people and places around you. This spell is great for empaths and could do wonders for anyone who deals with anxiety in public situations.

1. Choose black tourmaline for this spell. It should be one that calls to you and feels comfortable in the palm of your hand. Begin by cleansing it under running water, then patting it dry or leaving it in the sunlight.
2. Hold the crystal gently in your hands as you connect with its natural and pure energy. Feel the vibrations of your own energy pulsing against the crystal as the two energies combine and form a bond.

3. Say to the crystal, "I am protected from any negative energy that may try to enter this space. I feel calm, safe, and grounded." Repeat these affirmations as many times as necessary. While doing so, hold the vision in your mind's eye of yourself feeling safe and grounded (you can also recall a time when you felt safe and grounded, then relate it back to this moment). Keep this image in focus as you continue to feel the energy in your body form a tighter bond with the crystal in each passing second.

4. Place the black tourmaline near the front door to prevent unwanted energy from entering your space. You can use the crystal as a decorative item on an entry table or tuck it away, blending it into another piece of decor so that its placement isn't obvious. You can also place this near the entrance to your room or any space where energy protection is desired.

Manifesting Love Spell

For this spell, we are working at manifesting a pure and wholesome form of love. This love begins from within; thus, this spell is, at first, a self-love spell. When we learn to love ourselves, the whole world opens up to us. We must respect who we are and value what we can do before we can welcome others into our inner circle. If we cannot love who we are, then we cannot love others, which means that we will find it difficult to be loved. Once we can accept ourselves and love who we are, the spell will also manifest into growing friendships and romances. Our relationships will grow stronger, and we will be able to form those lasting and powerful bonds we have wished for with the people who enrich our lives for the better.

1. For this spell, we will use a rose quartz crystal. Cleanse the crystal under the moon's light by leaving it on your windowsill overnight. The moonlight is not only cleansing, but it is nurturing and compassionate. We want to fill the stone with this beautifully feminine energy, and for this reason, we will want to remove the rose quartz from the windowsill before it can capture too much sunlight in the morning.

2. Program your crystal by cradling it in the palm of your hands as you sit and meditate on a vision of yourself surrounded by love. Feel the warmth of acceptance, not only from those around you but from deep within (you can also recall a time when you felt this warmth and acceptance and connect it back to this moment). Keep hold of this vision and let it fill you as you say the following words. "I am

enough. I love myself and am worthy and capable of giving and receiving love."

3. Continue to allow the vision to take hold in your mind's eye as you feel the energy of the crystal radiate out and around your hands. At the same time, allow your intention to vibrate from your energy into the crystal, thus forming that intense bond. Repeat these affirmations as many times as needed until you feel as though the crystal has received your message. Know that the love you seek is already in existence during this meditation and will manifest into your life in its own way.

4. Keep the rose quartz with you at all times. Carry it in your purse or pocket as you go about your day. It can also be placed in a small crystal bag or pouch to protect it inside your purse. When you feel that you need a boost of self-love, you can hold the stone and think about the vision that you have of yourself.

Manifesting Abundance Spell

In this abundance spell, we are working at manifesting luck, courage, and clarity to gain wealth and prosperity in our lives. Sometimes the opportunities that we are seeking are right before us, and it takes a bit of courage and confidence to act upon these opportunities before

CRYSTAL WITCHCRAFT FOR BEGINNERS | 197

they pass us by. This spell will create the energy needed for you to stand up for yourself and take control of your success in your career or other entrepreneurial ventures. When we find success in our work, we are not only inspired by the creativity it took for us to achieve new goals, but we also obtain a level of self-confidence that can only be earned through hard work. With this spell, you will find gratitude in what you do as you will attract more wealth and abundance with ease.

1. For this spell, we will use pyrite to bring abundance and prosperity into our lives. We begin by cleansing the pyrite with sound. You can use things such as a bell, a singing bowl, drums, wind chimes, or even your own voice to cleanse the pyrite.

2. Take hold of the pyrite as you form a vision of yourself being successful in achieving the goals that you wish to achieve. How does it feel? Picture as many details as you can. Stay focused on your vision as you feel your energy vibrating toward the crystal from your body to your fingertips. See how you wish to be, and allow that energy and intention to flow deep into the crystal as you feel its energy pulsing. Allow the bond to form between your desires and the natural energy of the crystal.

3. Program the crystal by saying, "I am worthy of success. I am resourceful and capable of doing what needs to be done." You can add specific information about the success and prosperity you are after. Maybe it is a promotion that you are after. Specifically, stating it will help the crystal direct the energy toward your intention. Repeat the words until you feel that your energy and intentions have taken hold within the crystal. All the while, keep sight of yourself in your mind's eye, fully realizing the goals you have set and the benefits you will reap from finding confidence and success.

4. Place the pyrite somewhere in your office or workspace so that it can radiate out prosperous energies and help you remain focused on your goals. It will bring you clarity and certainty as you continue to focus on the successes that you wish to achieve. You can also keep the crystal in a pouch in your handbag or briefcase to further help you find prosperity during meetings, appointments, and when traveling.

USING CRYSTALS AS THEY ARE

As we discussed back in Chapter Three, crystals have the innate power that nature has gifted them. Because of this, it isn't necessary to program the crystal since it is well aware of what it can and cannot do. Sometimes we can trust in nature and utilize the crystals as they are. There's nothing wrong with this; sometimes, we can even skip cleansing our crystals as long as they feel positive and energetic when we pick them up.

For someone interested in crystal witchcraft, however, you will gain more insight and experience by working with your crystals on a deeper level. Understanding how to form bonds and enhance your crystals to raise their power is a fulfilling experience for anyone interested in crystal magic. It's likely that you are interested in more than simple healing because once we see what crystals can do, there's no turning back. Working with crystals is an enlightening experience; even using them exactly how we find them can bring empowerment and positive change like never before.

HOW TO USE CRYSTALS IN THE BEGINNING

Though a lot of this can be overwhelming for people unfamiliar with crystal witchcraft and the magic of natural healing, we still seek out the endless possibilities of the metaphysical world. Because of this, sometimes it's best to start simple and small until you are comfortable with using crystals in a more advanced setting.

You can start with one crystal, placing it in relevant spots as decoration in your home or office. Use the crystal immediately and experience how its energy feels as you work with it. You will form the bond you need to communicate better with the crystal in the future. For now, you'll be using it to empower your life straight away.

Even if you aren't sure what to do with it or whether or not it needs to be cleansed and programmed, it is wise to at least sit and meditate with it to form an energetic bond. This can take very little time, and after you are done, you can place it somewhere relevant to feel the effects of its healing powers.

SIMPLE AND QUICK CRYSTAL RITUALS

Sometimes the situations we are in call for simplicity. Whether it is because we are feeling overwhelmed or lacking time, or maybe we just prefer to keep things simple. Each of these rituals is designed to be done in only a matter of minutes. This means that they can help you in a pinch when you are dealing with something and need some guidance and clarity[1]. The best part about these rituals is that you can reuse them over and over however often you see fit. If you need a motivational boost every morning, use the motivation ritual to help you clear away the clutter and get things done.

Being consistent with your crystal practices, such as performing rituals, helps push away the unwanted thoughts that are weighing us down and confusing us as we try to seek out the goals we know will make us happy.

Motivation Ritual

Red Jasper

Remaining motivated is no easy task. Many of us have things we want to do, leading us to procrastinate on what we must do. By managing our time appropriately, we can accomplish anything, but it is all a matter of remaining motivated. Stay focused and achieve your goals by using this quick ritual anytime you feel that your motivation is faltering.

Holding the red jasper stone in your hands, ask it to guide you toward the part of your life that needs motivation. If you're already aware of what you want to work on, ask the red jasper to keep you grounded and focused as you pour your energy into the things that need to be done.

Creativity Ritual

Carnelian

Being creative is part of the uniqueness that humanity brings to the world. Our creativity can span across the humanities, the arts, and sometimes even just in the simple way that we express ourselves in our homes and with our clothing choices. Being able to use our imagination and inspire change is what helps us grow as a Collective Soul on this planet. When we experience a lack of creativity, inspiration, and self-expression, it can sometimes leave us feeling sad and anxious. This is because it keeps us from being true to ourselves.

Holding the carnelian stone in the palm of your hands, proclaim that you are creative, that you know your true self, and are capable of remaining true to who you are. This can become your mantra as you amplify the power within your crystal, and it, in turn, replenishes you with the creativity that you seek.

Clarity Ritual

Clear Quartz

Sometimes we have so many things going on in our busy lives that we have difficulties realizing what path we should be on. Even if we happen to know exactly what it is we're after, sometimes getting there can be just as tricky. By using clear quartz for this clarity spell, we are making a point to have the crystal help us understand whether we are on the right path and, if so, how to focus and get what we want.

Hold the clear quartz, and meditate with the intention to inspire clarity. Ask the clear quartz to show you the way, leading you toward the exact thing that you need to see at this moment.

Energy Ritual

Bloodstone

Sometimes we need a boost of energy, whether it be our midday wind down or something heavier that has been weighing on us, such as moving to a new home. Instead of relying on sugar and caffeine, we can ask crystals to help us break free from feeling lethargic so that we can rise up and seize the day. Bloodstone is great for this ritual because it is a stone of vitality, and it will literally help to get your blood pumping!

Hold the bloodstone in one hand as you move around vigorously for a minute. During this time, you'll want to allow the energy within the bloodstone to rise up through your arm and cascade over your body. This will warm you up and pull you out of whatever slump is keeping you from feeling that energy deep within. Keep moving as you feel the energy radiate throughout your core and back toward the bloodstone, again and again, until you have the motivation and desire to continue going on your own.

Stress Release Ritual

Blue Lace Agate

Don't we all have stress that we wish would just go away? Some people might confuse it with anxiety, but stress is what frustrates us and makes our bodies feel tense. Anxiety goes hand in hand because that is what happens afterward. When we are stressed out and cannot handle the things life hands us, we get so closed off and emotional that the only release is through jittery anxiety. This is a vicious cycle that we all deal with in our modern lives, and thankfully with the help of crystals, we can see an end to these bouts of stress.

Hold onto a blue lace agate in each hand (if you only have one, hold onto it with both hands), and take a moment to feel the relaxing energy as it washes over you completely. This will release the pent-up stress inside that has been causing you to feel tense and frustrated for too long. Envision this soothing energy flow around you as it calms and relieves all that is giving you trouble. This meditation can be as quick as only one minute, but you can choose to sit longer if you would like to allow the gentle energy of the blue lace agate to continue dissolving the stress you've been dealing with.

Relaxation Ritual

Amethyst

The queen of relaxation, amethyst, comes into this ritual ready to shut off the noise that is ever present in our minds. No matter what we are doing, it always seems like we could use a moment to ourselves. Maybe it's after work, after school, or even after a long day out shopping with the girls, but everyone needs a break. We need time for ourselves to unwind and let all of our emotions and feelings process in a healthy way.

Laying on your back, set an amethyst stone on your third eye chakra, the energy center located in the center of your forehead. Take a minute to feel the relaxing energy of the amethyst as it blankets your body, mind, and spirit with a healthy vibrational pulse of serenity. This ritual can also be done before going to sleep so that you can have a peaceful night's rest.

Sleep Ritual

Celestite

Speaking of sleep, when we don't get enough of it, we can be irritable and unable to focus. If we were able to get good quality sleep every night, we would not only be able to handle stressful days, but we would also have better motivation to accomplish the things that make us

206 | ESTELLE A. HARPER

feel good about ourselves. Celestite is the crystal of choice for this ritual, invoking dreaminess and whimsical vibes that allow us to let go of what is on our minds so we can sleep peacefully.

When you lay down for bed, hold the celestite crystal in your hands and allow its calming energy to flow around you. Whisper to yourself how you will sleep wonderfully and wake feeling refreshed and rejuvenated. Keep the crystal near your bed or beneath your pillow as you sleep.

TIPS FOR BEGINNERS

Embarking on this new journey can often be challenging, but it can also be exhilarating! The world of crystals is not only magical but it is scientifically proven to be beneficial to anyone anywhere. Crystals are a part of nature. They are non-invasive and non-discriminatory, filling us with health as they guide us toward success and protect us from negativity. Trust in nature, and it won't let you down. And with these few reminders, you'll feel even more at ease with the world of crystals.[2]

1. Know that all crystals can work in harmony with each other because they are an extension of this natural world. Remember that we are all connected by the web of energy on a cosmic

level and that everything flows rhythmically in our natural state as we work with crystals.

2. Trust your instincts when choosing a new crystal. If it feels like it might be too much for you, then take your time and wait until you are spiritually or physically ready to work with that new crystal.

3. Be open to the idea that the universe is guiding you in a way that you might not have expected. You may be accumulating crystals for something you are unaware of, but trust in the energy around you and the cosmos as it pushes you toward the path you were meant to walk.

4. Even though the universe will present you with opportunities and guidance, remember that you are empowered to do what is necessary for yourself. You have the energy within you to manifest whatever it is you desire. It is all a matter of learning to feel the energy within and around you and then recognizing when to manipulate that energy to your benefit.

5. Never fear when a beloved crystal goes missing. It might feel as though you have to scour the earth to retrieve it, but this is another part of the universe's guidance and the energetic web that ties us all together. You may have reasons for wanting that crystal, but the fact that it has

slipped out of your life may mean that you no longer need it, indicating that it may be time to shift focus onto something else that will bring you new joys and opportunities.

UNDERSTANDING AND MANAGING YOUR EXPECTATIONS

When we talk about using crystals to direct energy and make things happen, we enhance what we already have. Crystals work with the harmony that we already have, and this harmony exists within the balance of the energy surrounding us and flowing within us. It is our will to achieve things and prosper through the use of crystals, and we wish it to be so because the possibility is already there for it to happen.

In acknowledging this, we can also realize that we will only get out of our crystals what we put into them. We must put forth the time to create the bonds and cleanse and program our crystals for them to do what we wish. And more importantly, without these bonds and the understanding that we have of the energy of the cosmos, we cannot fully grasp what nature is capable of doing in the first place. We can only hope to achieve what we are willing to work for, and we cannot work for something that we do not understand. If you have high hopes and clear intentions, you must put in the work to honestly expect the results that you hope for.

Remember the law of attraction, where like attracts like. This means that for what you are seeking and what you hope to accomplish, you must be willing to match that same energy and passion as you strive toward these goals.

Manifestation is an active process that doesn't end the moment you program your crystal. You will need to be involved and actionable in this changing lifestyle that you are trying to create. Energy does not simply fabricate your wishes into existence; it requires nurturing and guidance; otherwise, it will falter. Like any other tangible goal you have set your eyes on, such as working hard to get a new job to create a better life for yourself, you must put in the work every day to see the results you are after.

We must remember along this journey that every single belief and thought we have can shape the reality before us. If we are adamant enough to use our mantras to tell ourselves that we can reach the dreams that seem so elusive, we will never hold ourselves back. However, suppose we continue to tell ourselves that we are incapable of doing something simply because of circumstances that appear to be out of our control. In that case, we will not only believe it, but it will also prevent the flow of positive changes in the reality around us. We no longer see ourselves rising above, but we learn to accept where we are and give up on the dreams that should rightfully be ours.

With crystals, we align our energy to become more aware of what is happening around us and how it affects our mental and our physical bodies. With this awareness comes a more open mind, and when we can see things clearly, we can plan and bring order into our chaotic lives. To rise above whatever's holding us back in this world, we must first allow ourselves to welcome the healing energy of the cosmos. It is at that point when we realize our full potential.

What you will experience will be different from what another person may experience. Our entire lives are highly individualized, and so will be the experience someone has with crystals and the healing energy of magic. You cannot base your success off of someone else's, and you must be honest about your current circumstances. Sometimes we have to remain a little grounded to find the life that best suits us. When we are humble, we can learn to enjoy what we have; that's when new doors open to allow us to find those elusive dreams that were right before our eyes this whole time.

We must be honest with our expectations when it comes to crystal healing because if we aren't willing to do what's necessary to bring our intentions into the real world, then we can't expect them to become true. The easiest way to see through each intention that you set forth is to continue to follow up with your crystals every day and repeat the words you used when programming them. By continuing to renew the bond you have with your crystals, you can refresh this energy and allow it to take hold. Before long, the seeds of your intentions will blossom into a fully grown manifestation, and what you wish to achieve will be ripe for harvest in no time.

FINAL WORDS

With this book, we have taken a deep dive into the healing powers of crystals. As a crystal witch, you have always had the power inside of you to make your intentions real. You can feel that call of nature telling you to listen to your inner voice and to do what you know is right for yourself. Through the healing powers of crystal witchcraft, you can now take your newfound knowledge and use it to empower your life and your practice as you grow closer to the crystals you adore.

Using crystals in your practice is all about the journey that you will take throughout your life. This journey can bring you many diverse choices, and crystals can help you find the clarity to understand what is best for you at every turn. Not only do they guide us through our uncertainties, but crystals allow us to clear away the negative energy and make room for a lighter and more productive energetic vibe. This is part of the journey. That beautiful journey that is all your own, now made easier thanks to crystals.

We began with a simple history of witchcraft as we took a deeper look at everything science has to offer. From quantum physics to the very nature of energy itself, we have examined every aspect of how healing occurs within our physical and mental bodies. This universal, cosmic energy that we are all bound to exists in both our physical world and in the spirit realm. Thanks to crystals, we now know that we can connect with our spiritual selves and our spirit guides and deities if we so wish, to enlighten us and enable us to see the magic and opportunity where we may not have before.

Energy healing is an enlightening experience, and even for people who aren't sure what to believe, it carries many benefits and proven results. We are all made of little molecules which compound to form matter. From this matter, we see our physical world, but beneath the surface lies a web of energy, connecting everything with the entirety of the universe. The healing we get from simply opening our eyes to the energy that surrounds us and flows within us is both immense and priceless. If you merely give it a try, I guarantee you'll never think of energy healing another way.

Our bodies are natural and organic entities within this vast world. When we take the time to reconnect to the nature that we sometimes stray from, we once again find the joys of natural healing and fulfillment. It's easy in our hectic lives to turn to convenience and take an easier route to comfort. Everything, from how we eat to where we travel, impacts the environment, the natural landscape around us, and our bodies and psyches. Taking time to bring nature into our lives once again is the key to finding that energy that we often feel has depleted from deep within.

As you continue on your journey, remember all the helpful advice that this book has provided you. If you have found even one thing to be helpful along your path in using crystals, consider spreading your joy to others by leaving a review of this book. It is my goal to guide other witches and anyone else interested in crystals through nature's incredible power and healing abilities. The best way that I can do that is with your help. As a reader of this book, your opinion matters a lot, not just to me but to other people who are seeking answers. Consider the good you can do simply by sharing your thoughts with a quick review. In only a few minutes, you could spread helpful knowledge to other people who are suffering and unaware of how to relieve the pain and sadness they deal with each day. This one act can go a long way for your own health as well. Knowing that you've helped others brings a certain amount of satisfaction that no other act can do. Not to mention the beautiful waves of karma you will be creating, ones that someday will come back to you.

I wish you the best on your journey to learning more about crystals as you bring them into your life, empowering your practice more with each passing day!

READY TO HELP LIGHT THE PATH FOR OTHERS?

No matter where we are on our spiritual journey, we all need guidance... and you're in the perfect position to offer it.

Simply by leaving your honest opinion of this book on Amazon, you can help other people find the guidance they need to unlock their inner power and discover the incredible strength of crystals.

I'm so grateful for your support... and I just know thousands of other readers will be too. Our individual energy is powerful... but when we share it, it's a force to be reckoned with.

Scan the QR code here:

9

BONUS CHAPTER: INTRO TO EXPANDING YOUR CRYSTAL WITCHCRAFT JOURNEY

*a*fter you have learned from this book and found the practices that offer you fulfillment and satisfaction in your life, you may want to expand on this knowledge and grow deeper into your magic with crystals. As a beginner, you may eventually seek out new information and new experiences to enhance what you've already learned. With a good hold of the basic principles involved in crystal magic, you can take the next step and truly embrace the crystal witchcraft journey!

EXPANDING YOUR CRYSTAL COLLECTION

One of the best parts of crystal work is that there are hundreds of fascinating types of crystals available to use in your practice, not to mention the endless speci-mens in their unique shapes and colors. After building your core collection from the thirty-four crystals recommended in this book, you can expand into other types of crystals that offer even more unique properties.

Crystals are diverse and fascinating in their raw form, and it is important to know that many of them come in a variety of colors and patterns as well. Agate and jasper are two of the most commonly used stones, with numerous versions in beautiful designs and mesmer-izing colors. Each one of them influences a different energy center, and they do different things for the mind, body, and spirit. They can also be used in your home and office to invoke specific energies and vibrations.

CONSISTENT RITUALS TO EASE THE MIND

Crystal witches who take the time to understand their crystals will soon want more advanced rituals and activities that involve those crystals. With a solid bond between yourself and your crystals, you will want to continue to amplify the energy in and around you as you learn more about the power that they hold. After you have the basic knowledge of spells and rituals with the help of the short rituals and the five-step spells that we discussed in Chapter Eight, you can branch out and use more advanced techniques in the future.

Not only do we want to learn and grow with our crystals by advancing our knowledge with each new ritual, but we will also want to remain consistent by practicing rituals on a weekly, if not daily, basis. The more you repeat the process, the better your mind and body will align. Rituals allow us to take a moment to care for ourselves, enabling us to be more mindful of who we are in relation to the universe. Having a daily practice, even if it is only for a moment, will help you learn to practice self-love and self-expression in a healthy way.

Everything starts with a thought, and those thoughts are incredibly powerful. When we remove the clutter and allow our thoughts to hone in on what matters most, we find that inner motivation to walk the path that personally benefits us. Our minds can heal better than anything else, and at their peak, we find enlightenment. This carefree and relaxed achievement of enlightenment comes from consistent rituals and repetitive hard work, which allows our minds to relax and step away from the pressures that are weighing us down.

222 | ESTELLE A. HARPER

CREATING A PERSONAL SPACE IN YOUR LIFE FOR CRYSTALS

With these advanced practices, you can bring your love of crystals into your home with rituals, decor, and mindfulness for your personal growth. For each of these new practices, you may need additional materials and tools, and you will most likely want to expand on your crystal collection. Remember that taking your time and using what is most comfortable for you is how you will find yourself on this journey and stay true to who you are. Loving yourself is a vital skill to learn, and some people may take longer because they have a tendency to please others. When it comes to your safe space and your home, it is wise to be patient with your collection. Whether it involves crystals or other elements of style, you will want to take the time to listen to your inner voice so that your true spirit can shine.

Sanctuaries

A dedicated area for your crystals and the practice of witchcraft is a big step in bringing magic into your everyday life. This place is specifically for you to be able to come back to your crystals whenever you need to bond their energy with your own. This can be a private area of your home or garden where you feel safe and comfortable practicing the spiritual or metaphysical aspects of crystal magic. It is a personal place, and because of that, it is highly individualized depending on the person who designs it. It should reflect all of you, inside and out, and all of your favorite things, dreams, and aspirations.

Within your sanctuary, you should be able to practice self-care, worship the deities that you wish, and communicate with your spirit guides. This space will be an area for you to perform rituals and meditate, and you may even want to include peaceful, mindful practices such as yoga.

Your sanctuary can be a part of another room that you already enjoy, like maybe the corner of your bedroom. It's important, however, that you choose a spot that is away from things that remind you of unwanted energy or feelings. For instance, you might not want to use the same desk that you use to manage your finances as your sanctuary. Sometimes we have difficulties in our finances, which can burden our home and our psyche. In this example, keeping your crystals in a neutral place will help you maintain the type of energy that you seek.

On that note, the sanctuary should not be placed where a lot of people pass by because their energy can pour into the space and alter the way your crystals behave. This can also affect the rituals and spells that you choose to enact, especially if you are using the space to create them.

It's very important that you use your intuition to discover a place that feels most comfortable and has the right energy for what you wish to achieve. Some witches are energetic and full of vibrancy, and their space reflects that. Others may choose quiet spaces and keep their areas minimal. The room in which she chose to place her sanctuary is a part of this as well because a witch who likes peacefulness and simplicity may choose a corner of her bedroom and use something as simple as a bookshelf to keep her things.

Altars

An altar is a space where you can perform the actual ritual or spell itself. Sometimes this is as simple as lighting a candle in the morning and saying a prayer. You can also set out a few items as an offering to a deity. Crystal witches enjoy placing crystals all around their altar to amplify the energy that will be used within a spell or ritual. Oftentimes altars are included within the sanctuary, but an altar can also be separate. It can be grand or minimal and is all up to the witch and how they want to perform their magic.

Altars have a religious affiliation, but just because they hold that history, it doesn't mean they are only for that purpose. An altar is nothing more than a small flat space that we use to place our things and chant the intentions of our spells. It's very similar to saying a prayer, where we communicate our intentions to the universe, particular deities, or our spirit guides. An altar is also great for people who simply want to use crystals for healing purposes and nothing more. It is a safe space for you to set out your crystals where they will not be messed with and can be preserved with their natural energy after being cleansed.

To create an altar that would reflect your own way of practicing witchcraft, there are a few steps that we can review to make the process easy and fun. Sometimes diving into a big project like building an altar can seem overwhelming, but when we take it step by step, we learn to express ourselves as we make our spaces our own.

Decide on what the purpose is for your altar. Will you use it for meditation, organizing your crystal collection, or perhaps to perform the rituals you wish to include in your practice? Once you identify the purpose, you will know what size of space you will need to encompass everything you wish to include.

Choose a space with an elevated surface that can be entirely dedicated to the altar. This can be the top of a short bookshelf, a small table, a nightstand, or a shelf on the wall. These are all examples; you may find something else that will work perfectly for you.

Pick a featured item that will be the main focal point of your altar. Some people do not choose to do this, as they like to accumulate various objects of similar size to build an eclectic altar. Personally, I prefer using a focal item as it helps me create the aesthetic I'm going for with the rest of my altar space. We can use a large candle, for example, to create the centerpiece for the altar. Around the candle, we can place herbs or other plant material, followed by our favorite crystals. You can also use a large-sized geode as a focal point and place small candles around it. There truly are hundreds of different ways that we can create an altar to reflect the things we love most about magic.

After the centerpiece is chosen, decorate the remaining space with whatever is meaningful and valuable to you. These items become sacred to your altar and your practice as a witch. You might have found pinecones on a walk and would like to place them around your altar. You may also have small knick-knacks that hold special meaning and would like to include them. Whatever the case, just remember to take your time and add the things that are important to you and that hold the energy you feel most comfortable with.

Creating a crystal magic-themed altar is another wonderful way to form a deeper bond with the crystals you use regularly. We can choose a crystal that is charged with the intention to empower the energy of your altar and all the rituals that will come in the future as the focal piece. Adding clear quartz and selenite to the altar will bring cleansing energy and allow the altar to stay true to the energy that you have designed it for. You can also place your crystal cleansing bowl or small bag nearby to keep the crystals clear from unwanted energies. You can decorate the remaining space of your altar with various crystals from your collection. Finally, you can add a crystal grid to your altar to bring about specific energies and intentions.

ADDING PERSONALITY TO YOUR SANCTUARY OR ALTAR

Perhaps the most fulfilling aspect of creating a space for your practice is to design and decorate it to reflect your inner personality. As a witch who adores all the fun little magical decorations there are in this world, this is something that I absolutely love! We can get creative as we design our spaces, bringing in different things that we enjoy about nature and the world around us. Everything you choose brings energy to your space, so be very mindful of the energy flowing in and out of these objects before adding them to your collection.

Decorations can vary across all different shapes and colors. Feel free to use anything you want when decorating your space and adding items to fill the energy in your sanctuary and around your altar. Not all elements need to come from nature, even if you are a nature witch at heart. We can use things such as old letters and postcards that hold sentimental value, photographs, souvenirs, and trinkets. These things are even more important to your space if they have a connection to a person or a place that means a lot to you. For example, you might have an old necklace of a past relative. That relative might be a spirit guide to you now, and by keeping that memento in your space, you have a direct connection to that person and their lasting energy.

We can use the senses to help us decorate our spaces as well. Some people love certain smells and can use candles and incense to fill their space. We may want to use bells or other small items that create soothing and peaceful sounds. And, of course, decorating with our crystals can bring diverse shapes and colors into our space, enhancing the aesthetic of our overall sanctuary or altar.

CRYSTAL GRIDS

A crystal grid is a powerful technique that crystal witches use to harness specific energy and manifest clear intentions. Just like how an altar is often placed in a sanctuary, a crystal grid is an addition to your personal space. Some grids can be elaborate and contain many crystals, while others might only have as few as four. This all depends on what you have created it for, and you will want to find a good spot within your sanctuary or near your altar to keep it (it can also be part of your altar or the centerpiece of it).

A crystal grid is a purposeful and thoughtful arrangement of crystals that hold a collective intention. Sometimes we set out our crystals in no specific order or pattern, and these designs are not necessarily considered crystal grids. A crystal grid is when crystals are placed within a specific pattern, allowing each one to feed off the next, causing the collective to become amplified with the intention you have set.

Not only does the grid amplify your intentions to help manifest what you seek, but it also uses sacred geometry, which is found everywhere, including nature, the human body, architecture, and even space!

To create the grid itself, you will first want to designate a central crystal that will sit in the middle of the surrounding crystals. The center crystal holds the main intention and becomes the focal point for the grid's energy. This crystal and the intention you have set forth become the two most important aspects of the grid itself.

With the remaining crystals you've chosen for your grid, you will create a geometric shape around the center crystal to support and amplify the intention. The best way to allow a crystal grid to do its work is to find a space where it cannot be interrupted or deconstructed before you are ready to dismantle it. Aside from a space where the grid will not get bothered, you will also need the center crystal and at least three other crystals for support, and you may want to use a crystal wand or clear quartz crystal with a point for activation. Other options include using an athame or personal wands made from different materials such as twigs. Some witches also opt to simply use their pointer finger to activate their grids.

When designing your crystal grid, you will want to have a clear purpose and intention in mind. This will impact the type of crystals you choose, especially the center crystal that will hold the intention itself. You will want to have a crystal that aligns with the energy you are trying to create, such as using rose quartz to bring about love. After you have your center crystal, you will want to choose other crystals that will align with this energy and amplify the intention. For example, if you are using rose quartz, you might use other pink and purple stones to help build this intention of love. Also, using clear quartz as a substitute for any crystal is a great choice because clear quartz can amplify any meaning of any other stone available. Tumbled stones are excellent for crystal grids, but any crystal form/shape will work just the same.

Constructing Your Own Crystal Grid

To prepare for the grid, cleanse your crystals in the manner best suited for each one so that the crystal's natural energy and physical nature remain intact. Design the crystal grid in the arrangement you wish to use, or you can use a printout of a popular one. Printouts can be traced onto wooden surfaces and marked out on cloth or in sand. Using the elements to your benefit, you can choose different mediums for this grid layout to further amplify the energy of your intention. Once you've got all your materials together, you can select the space where you would like to set up your crystal grid.

As you build the grid itself, you will want to be in the right mood for the energy you wish to produce. For example, suppose you happen to be in a bad mood from something that happened during the day. You may want

232 | ESTELLE A. HARPER

to refrain from building your crystal grid until you've had time to reduce the negative emotions and energy from within yourself and your physical body. You can use meditation to release these unwanted energies and get into the right state of mind for the intention you wish to create. You can also bring forth the right energies by lighting candles, playing music, or using some of the quick rituals discussed in Chapter Eight.

When you feel that you have the right mindset to bring about your intention with a clear focus, begin by setting the supporting crystals onto the grid. Once they are in place, you can program your center crystal with your intention. Just as we did in Chapter Seven, hold onto your crystal and speak your intention as you visualize what you wish to manifest coming true. Remember to hold that vision as long as you can as you allow it to fully come to light, all while the energies of your body and the crystal are intermingling. Once this intention is programmed into the center crystal, you can place that crystal into the middle of your grid. Now we can activate the grid with our wands; as we do this, we will want to continue that vision of our intention becoming real.

With the wand (or your pointer finger), hover over each crystal, starting with the center. Visualize connecting each surrounding crystal's energy to the center crystal, one at a time, with the vision of your intention at the forefront of your mind. Go over each crystal and individually connect them to the center crystal while you imagine how it would feel to manifest your new reality. The more specific your intention is, the better the manifestation will fit what you're hoping to achieve.

Important Points for Starting

It's easy to get carried away with crystal grids when first starting out. Their potential for amplified power is appealing, but we must be careful not to overwhelm ourselves during the first few attempts. Not only can we get weighed down by the promise of untold power, but excessive crystals all working toward different things can pull our energy in separate directions. Starting out small and simple, one grid at a time, is the key to getting grids right in the beginning.

The most important part of the crystal grid is the relationship between your center crystal and the intentions you've set. After that, you must keep in mind the law of attraction and how similar things come together.

While the grid is in place, you might find some clarity about the situation, indicating that it may be time to move on. You have to be honest with your expectations and allow for the possibility that things may not go as you have hoped. This is all part of the divine energy that is guiding you toward the path you should be on. Don't let your desires occupy your mind unless they bring you closer to the happiness you seek.

Using other crystals to meditate and confirm your intentions is wise, and you can do this near your crystal grid to keep the energy full and the vibrations high. Find inspiration in everything and let your creativity flow with your designs and crystal choices.

Frequently Asked Questions About Crystal Grids

How long should the crystal grid be kept?

Crystal grids can be wired together and kept permanently, depending on their purpose. Grids should be left in place for at least one week to allow the intention to take root. You can revisit the grid and reaffirm your intentions during the week by using your mantras and visualization techniques. When you feel that the grid has served its purpose, you can dismantle it and cleanse the stones.

What is the fewest number of crystals used in a crystal grid?

Using at least four crystals will help you construct a geometric crystal grid with plenty of amplified energy. By using a center crystal with three surrounding it, you can easily create a pyramid of energy to work with your intentions.

What types of crystal shapes should be used?

For the center crystal, using something with a point will work best for amplification. For the surrounding stones, use raw or tumbled stones that align with the energies of the center stone. If you wish to direct specific energy from the surrounding stones to the center stone, you can also use pointed crystals with all tips directing energy toward the center.

REFERENCES

"5 Things Everyone Needs to Know About Energy Healing, Growth Wellness Therapy". Growth Wellness Therapy. March 4, 2020. https://www.growthwellnesstherapy.com/our-blog/5-things-everyone-needs-to-know-about-energy-healing

"Agate Meaning: Healing Properties & Everyday Uses". Tiny Rituals. https://tinyrituals.co/blogs/tiny-rituals/agate-meaning-healing-properties-everyday-uses

"Aventurine Meaning: Healing Properties & Everyday Uses". Tiny Rituals. https://tinyrituals.co/blogs/tiny-rituals/aventurine-meaning-healing-properties-everyday-uses

"Carnelian Meaning: Healing Properties & Everyday Uses". Tiny Rituals. https://tinyrituals.co/blogs/tiny-rituals/carnelian-meaning-healing-properties

"Celestite Meaning: Healing Properties & Everyday Uses". Tiny Rituals. https://tinyrituals.co/blogs/tiny-rituals/celestite-meaning-healing-properties-everyday-uses

"Chrysocolla Meaning: Healing Properties & Everyday Uses". Tiny Rituals. https://tinyrituals.co/blogs/tiny-rituals/chrysocolla-meaning-healing-properties-everyday-uses

"Citrine Meaning: Healing Properties & Everyday Uses". Tiny Rituals. https://tinyrituals.co/blogs/tiny-rituals/citrine-meaning-healing-properties

"Clear Quartz Meaning: Healing Properties & Uses". Tiny Rituals. https://tinyrituals.co/blogs/tiny-rituals/clear-quartz-meaning-healing-properties-uses

"Fluorite Meaning: Healing Properties & Everyday Uses". Tiny Rituals. https://tinyrituals.co/blogs/tiny-rituals/fluorite-meaning-healing-properties-everyday-uses

"Garnet Meaning: Healing Properties & Everyday Uses". Tiny Rituals.

https://tinyrituals.co/blogs/tiny-rituals/garnet-meaning-healing-properties

"Healing Your Mother (or Father) Wound". Dharma Wisdom. Assessed May 1, 2022. https://dharmawisdom.org/healing-your-mother-or-father-wound/

"History of Witches". History.Com. Assessed May 3, 2022. https://www.history.com/topics/folklore/history-of-witches

"Jade Meaning: Healing Properties & Everyday Uses. Tiny Rituals". https://tinyrituals.co/blogs/tiny-rituals/jade-meaning-healing-properties-everyday-uses

"Kyanite Meaning: Healing Properties & Everyday Uses". Tiny Rituals. https://tinyrituals.co/blogs/tiny-rituals/kyanite-meaning-healing-properties-everyday-uses

"Labradorite Meaning: All The Healing Properties & Uses You NEED To Know". Tiny Rituals. https://tinyrituals.co/blogs/tiny-rituals/labradorite-meaning-all-the-properties-you-need-to-know

"Lapis Lazuli Meaning: Healing Properties & Everyday Uses". Tiny Rituals. https://tinyrituals.co/blogs/tiny-rituals/lapis-lazuli-meaning-healing-properties

"Lepidolite Meaning: Healing Properties & Everyday Use". Tiny Rituals. https://tinyrituals.co/blogs/tiny-rituals/lepidolite-meaning-healing-properties-everyday-use

"Malachite Meaning: Healing Properties & Everyday Uses". Tiny Rituals. https://tinyrituals.co/blogs/tiny-rituals/malachite-meaning-healing-properties

"Moonstone Meaning: Healing Properties & Everyday Uses". Tiny Rituals. https://tinyrituals.co/blogs/tiny-rituals/moonstone-meaning-healing-properties-everyday-uses

"Peridot Meaning: Healing Properties & Everyday Uses". Tiny Rituals. https://tinyrituals.co/blogs/tiny-rituals/peridot-meaning-stone-guide-healing-properties

"Pyrite Meaning: Healing Properties & Everyday Uses". Tiny Rituals. https://tinyrituals.co/blogs/tiny-rituals/pyrite-meaning-healing-properties-everyday-uses

"Red Jasper Meaning: Healing Properties & Everyday Uses". Tiny Rituals. https://tinyrituals.co/blogs/tiny-rituals/red-jasper-meaning-healing-properties-and-everyday-uses

"Rhodonite Meaning: Healing Properties & Everyday Uses". Tiny Rituals. https://tinyrituals.co/blogs/tiny-rituals/rhodonite-meaning-healing-properties-everyday-uses

"Rose Quartz Meaning: Healing Properties And Everyday Uses". Tiny Rituals. https://tinyrituals.co/blogs/tiny-rituals/rose-quartz-meaning-healing-properties-and-everyday-uses

"Selenite Meaning: Healing Properties & Everyday Uses". Tiny Rituals. https://tinyrituals.co/blogs/tiny-rituals/selenite-meaning-healing-properties-everyday-uses

"Smoky Quartz Meaning: Healing Properties & Everyday Uses". Tiny Rituals. https://tinyrituals.co/blogs/tiny-rituals/smoky-quartz-meaning-healing-properties-everyday-uses

"The Illusion of Reality: The Scientific Proof That Everything is Energy and Reality Isn't Real". http://www.esalq.usp.br/lepse/imgs/conteudo_thumb/The-Illusion-of-Reality---The-Scientific-Proof-That-Everything-is-Energy-and-Reality-Isnt-Real.pdf

"The Meaning of Hematite: What You Need To Know - Healing Properties & More!". Tiny Rituals. https://tinyrituals.co/blogs/tiny-rituals/hematite-meaning-healing-properties-stone-guide

"The Meaning Of Sodalite: The Ultimate Guide". Tiny Rituals. https://tinyrituals.co/blogs/tiny-rituals/sodalite-meaning-stone-guide-healing-properties

"Tigers Eye Meaning: Secrets & Healing Properties Revealed". Tiny Rituals. https://tinyrituals.co/blogs/tiny-rituals/tiger-eye-meaning-and-uses

"Turquoise Meaning: Physical, Emotional, & Spiritual Healing Properties". Tiny Rituals. https://tinyrituals.co/blogs/tiny-rituals/turquoise-howlite-meaning-healing-properties-and-everyday-uses

"Why Do Witches Ride Brooms?". History.Com. Assessed May 3, 2022. https://www.history.com/news/why-witches-fly-on-brooms

Abram, Christy Lynn, How To Clean & Store Your Crystals—Plus A 6-

Step Programming Technique, Mind Body Green, June 14, 2021, https://www.mindbodygreen.com/0-14887/how-to-clear-activate-store-your-crystals.html

Allard, Syama. "5 Things to Know About Karma and Reincarnation". Hindu American Foundation. September 4, 2020. https://www.hinduamerican.org/blog/5-things-to-know-about-karma-and-reincarnation

Amazonite Meaning: Healing Properties & Everyday Uses, Tiny Rituals, https://tinyrituals.co/blogs/tiny-rituals/amazonite-meaning-stone-guide-healing-properties

Amethyst Meaning: Everything You NEED To Know - Healing Properties & Everyday Uses, Tiny Rituals, https://tinyrituals.co/blogs/tiny-rituals/amethyst-meaning-healing-properties-and-everyday-uses

Amsen, Eva, What is a Crystal?, Let's Talk Science, July 19, 2019, https://letstalkscience.ca/educational-resources/stem-in-context/what-a-crystal

Angelite Meaning: Healing Properties & Everyday Uses, Tiny Rituals, https://tinyrituals.co/blogs/tiny-rituals/angelite-meaning-healing-properties-everyday-uses

Askinosie, Heather, 8 Ways To Use Crystals In Your Everyday Routine, Mind Body Green, January 31, 2020, https://www.mindbodygreen.com/0-23590/8-lesserknown-ways-to-use-crystals-in-your-everyday-routine.html

Askinosie, Heather, A Room-by-Room Guide to Using Crystals for the Home, Energy Muse, January 18, 2019, https://www.energymuse.com/blog/using-crystals-for-the-home-and-interior-design

Black Tourmaline Meaning: Healing Properties & Everyday Uses, Tiny Rituals, https://tinyrituals.co/blogs/tiny-rituals/black-tourmaline-meaning-healing-properties-and-everyday-uses

Bloodstone Meaning: Healing Properties & Everyday Uses, Tiny Rituals, https://tinyrituals.co/blogs/tiny-rituals/bloodstone-meaning-healing-properties-everyday-uses

Brady, James E., and Prufer, Keith M., Caves and Crystalmancy: Evidence for the Use of Crystals in Ancient Maya Religion, The

Journal of Anthropological Research, The University of Chicago Press, Spring 1999, https://www.jstor.org/stable/3630980

Carlos, Kristine D., Crystal Healing Practices in the Western World and Beyond, University of Central Florida, STARS, 2018, https://stars. library.ucf.edu/cgi/viewcontent.cgi?article=1283&context= honorstheses

Chee, Chermaine, How To Cleanse Crystals: 4 Ways To Cleanse Crystals, Truly Experiences, September 27, 2021, https://trulyexperi ences.com/blog/how-to-cleanse-crystals/

Davis, Faith, How Energy Moves Through the Chakra System, Cosmic Cuts, January 28, 2021, https://cosmiccuts.com/blogs/healing-stones-blog/chakra-system

Egnew, Thomas R. "The Meaning Of Healing: Transcending Suffering". Annals of Family Medicine. May 2005. https://www.annfammed. org/content/annalsfm/3/3/255.full.pdf

Haley, Jolene. "Crystal Healing, History and Science Behind this Ancient Practice". We're Wild. October 19, 2018. https://werewild. co/crystal-healing-history-and-science-behind-this-ancient-practice/

Harvard Medical School, How the Placebo Effect May Help You, Harvard Health Publishing, May 1, 2017, https://www.health. harvard.edu/mind-and-mood/how-the-placebo-effect-may-help-you

The Meaning Of Aquamarine: Everything You Wanted To Know, Tiny Rituals, https://tinyrituals.co/blogs/tiny-rituals/aquamarine-mean ing-stone-guide-healing-properties

How Do Gemstones Form?, Gem Rock Auctions, https://www. gemrockauctions.com/learn/technical-information-on-gemstones/ how-do-gemstones-form

How To Cleanse Crystals: 9 Crucial Practices You Need To Know, Tiny Rituals, https://tinyrituals.co/blogs/tiny-rituals/how-to-cleanse-crystals

How To Program Quartz Crystals, Sacred Gemstone, https://www. sacredgemstone.com/pages/programming-quartz-crystals

Khan, Nina, 11 Easy One-Minute Crystal Rituals That Will Help You

Attract All The Good Vibes, Bustle, December 4, 2018, https://www.bustle.com/p/11-easy-one-minute-crystal-rituals-to-try-even-if-youre-a-crystal-newbie-13242074

Marino, Caitlin, and The Goop Wellness Team. "Working Through Karmic Wounds". Goop Wellness. Assessed May 1, 2022. https://goop.com/wellness/spirituality/healing-karmic-wounds/

Obsidian Meaning: Healing Properties & Everyday Uses, Tiny Rituals, https://tinyrituals.co/blogs/tiny-rituals/obsidian-meaning-healing-properties-everyday-uses

Scialla, Janelle, A Brief History of Crystals and Healing, Crystal Age, https://www.crystalage.com/crystal_information/crystal_history/

Team Elle, Healing Crystals - What Are They And How Should You Use Them?, Elle Magazine, July 5, 2021, https://www.elle.com/uk/life-and-culture/culture/articles/a31572/what-are-healing-crystals-how-to-use-them/

Trivedi, Mahendra, "Biofield Energy Signals, Energy Transmission and Neutrinos". American Journal of Modern Physics. 2016. https://www.infona.pl/resource/bwmeta1.element.ID-b851ae2e-c93c-4b39-8416-bb6903391712

Yasay, Dominic, Your Quick Guide to Crystal Shapes, Meanings, and Uses, StoneBridge Imports, July 30, 2021 https://stonebridgeimports.ca/a/635-your-quick-guide-to-crystal-shapes-meanings-and-uses

Yoga, Int J. "Energy Medicine". The National Library of Medicine. January-June 2010. https://www.ncbi.nlm.nih.gov/pmc/articles/PMC2952118/

Stardust, Lisa. 2021. "Here's What It Means To Be A Real-Life Witch In 2021". Instyle. https://www.instyle.com/lifestyle/witch-meaning-myths.

"Medieval World: Crime And Punishment - Including Witchcraft". 2022. Matthew Flinders Girls Secondary College. https://mfgsc-vic.libguides.com/c.php?g=916765&p=6609523.

Editors, History.com. 2011. "Salem Witch Trials". HISTORY. https://www.history.com/topics/colonial-america/salem-witch-trials.

Howes, Dr Hetta. 2015. "Medieval Magic: A Brief History | Historyextra". *Historyextra.Com.* https://www.historyextra.com/period/medieval/a-brief-history-of-medieval-magic/.

The witches' cookery. 2021. *How To Know What Witch You Are | 20 Types Of Witches*. Video. https://www.youtube.com/watch?v=r_7riS3U VUY&ab_channel=Thewitches%27cookery.

Editors, History.com. 2022. "Wicca". *HISTORY.* https://www.history.com/topics/religion/wicca.

HearthWitch. 2019. *Types Of Witches ∥ Witchcraft 101.* Video. https://www.youtube.com/watch?v=d48uaYMTtY0&ab_channel=Hearth Witch.

Young, Olivia. 2020. "Witchcraft For Beginners: History, Types, And Meaning". *Conscious Items.* https://consciousitems.com/blogs/life style/witchcraft-for-beginners-history-types-and-meaning.

Items, Conscious. 2022. *The Modern Mystic Guide.* Ebook. Conscious Items. Accessed September 18. https://cdn.shopify.com/s/files/1/2194/4189/files/The_Modern_Mystic_Guide___Desktop.pdf?v=1603801659.

The Green Witch. 2019. *What Kind Of Witch Are You? ∥ Nine Types Of Witches ∥ Witchcraft 101.* Video. https://www.youtube.com/watch?v=zf_GowlOkgI&ab_channel=TheGreenWitch.

The Mindful Mage. 2021. *21 Different Types Of Witches.* Video. https://www.youtube.com/watch?v=1Jui7Y4cnfU&ab_channel=TheMind fulMage.

vulpix. 2018. *Types Of Witches!.* Video. https://www.youtube.com/watch?v=jFL_pgD22ZA&ab_channel=vulpix.

Herstik, Gabriela. 2019. "Modern Witches From Japan To Mexico Explain What The Craft Means Today". *3 Modern Witches From Different Cultures Explain What The Craft Means Today.* https://www.vogue.co.uk/arts-and-lifestyle/article/modern-witches-experience.

Grossman, Pam. 2019. "Yes, Witches Are Real. I Know Because I Am One". *Time.* https://time.com/5597693/real-women-witches/.

Egnew, Thomas R. 2009. "Suffering, Meaning, And Healing: Challenges Of Contemporary Medicine". *Annfammed.Org.* https://www.annfammed.org/content/annalsfm/7/2/170.full.pdf.

Warber, Sara L., Rosalyn L. Bruyere, Ken Weintrub, and Paul Dieppe.

2015. "A Consideration Of The Perspectives Of Healing Practitioners On Research Into Energy Healing". *Practitioners' Perspectives Of Energy Healing*. https://journals.sagepub.com/doi/pdf/10.7453/gahmj.2015.014.suppl.

Bennett, Elizabeth. 2019. "Feeling Stressed And Stuck At Home? Give Remote Healing A Try". *Healthline*. https://www.healthline.com/health/mind-body/remote-energy-healing-does-it-actually-work.

Beri, Kavita. 2018. "A Future Perspective For Regenerative Medicine: Understanding The Concept Of Vibrational Medicine". *National Library Of Medicine*. https://www.ncbi.nlm.nih.gov/pmc/articles/PMC5859346/.

Baron, Marci. 2020. "What Everyone Should Know About Energy Healing". *Mbgmindfulness*. https://www.mindbodygreen.com/0-23890/what-everyone-should-know-about-energy-healing.html.

Rubik, Beverly, David Muehsam, Richard Hammerschlag, and Shamini Jain. 2015. "Biofield Science And Healing: History, Terminology, And Concepts". *National Library Of Medicine*. https://www.ncbi.nlm.nih.gov/pmc/articles/PMC4654789/.

Zhang, Ming, Mohamed Moalin, Lily Vervoort, Zheng Wen Li, and Guido Haenen. 2019. "Connecting Western And Eastern Medicine From An Energy Perspective". *National Library Of Medicine*. https://www.ncbi.nlm.nih.gov/pmc/articles/PMC6470590/.

Blakeway, Jill, and The Goop Wellness Team. 2022. "The Science And Mystery Of Energy Healing". *Goop*. Accessed September 19. https://goop.com/ca-en/wellness/spirituality/science-of-energy-healing/.

Marino, Caitlin, and The Goop Wellness Team. 2022. "Working Through Karmic Wounds". *Goop*. Accessed September 19. https://goop.com/wellness/spirituality/healing-karmic-wounds/.

Herstik, Gabriela. 2022. "Healing Your Shadows: Inviting The Light In To Heal Karmic Wounds — The Hoodwitch". *The Hoodwitch*. Accessed September 19. https://www.thehoodwitch.com/blog/2016/4/26/healing-your-shadows-inviting-the-light-in-to-heal-karmic-wounds.

Jones, Dr. Logan. 2022. "3 Essential Tips On How To Heal Emotional

Wounds And Trauma - Claritytherapynyc.Com". *Claritytherapyny-c.Com.* Accessed September 19. https://www.claritytherapynyc.com/how-to-heal-emotional-wounds/.

Jain, Sarika. 2020. "A Simple Practice To Heal Your Karmic Wounds". *Sarika Jain.* https://sarikajain.com/a-simple-practice-to-heal-your-karmic-wounds/.

Faith, Davis. 2022. "12 Root Chakra Stones | Stability, Vitality & Grounding | Cosmic Cuts©". *Cosmic Cuts.* Accessed September 19. https://cosmiccuts.com/blogs/healing-stones-blog/root-chakra-stones.

Faith, Davis. 2022. "Sacral Charka Stones: 8 Crystals For Enjoyment, Creativity & Emotional". *Cosmic Cuts.* Accessed September 19. https://cosmiccuts.com/blogs/healing-stones-blog/sacral-charka-stones.

Faith, Davis. 2022. "8 Solar Plexus Chakra Stones For Transformation & Personal Power". *Cosmic Cuts.* Accessed September 19. https://cosmiccuts.com/blogs/healing-stones-blog/solar-plexus-chakra-stones.

Faith, Davis. 2022. "Heart Chakra Stones: 12 Crystals For Love, Connection & Wholeness". *Cosmic Cuts.* Accessed September 19. https://cosmiccuts.com/blogs/healing-stones-blog/heart-chakra-stones.

Faith, Davis. 2022. "12 Throat Chakra Stones For Expression, Communication & Authenticity". *Cosmic Cuts.* Accessed September 19. https://cosmiccuts.com/blogs/healing-stones-blog/throat-chakra-stones.

Faith, Davis. 2022. "Third Eye Chakra Stones: 13 Crystals For Intuition, Wisdom, & Awakenin". *Cosmic Cuts.* Accessed September 19. https://cosmiccuts.com/blogs/healing-stones-blog/third-eye-chakra-stones.

Faith, Davis. 2022. "Crown Chakra Stones: 10 Crystals For Unity, Enlightenment & Spiritual". *Cosmic Cuts.* Accessed September 19. https://cosmiccuts.com/blogs/healing-stones-blog/crown-chakra-stones.

Faith, Davis. 2022. "How To Use Crystals For The Best Chakra Healing | Cosmic Cuts©". *Cosmic Cuts*. Accessed September 19. https://cosmiccuts.com/blogs/healing-stones-blog/how-to-use-crystals-for-the-best-chakra-healing.

Broverman, Jessica, and Weelunk Staff. 2020. "The History And Modern Application Of Witchcraft And Crystals". *Weelunk*. https://weelunk.com/history-modern-application-witchcraft-crystals/.

"The Science Behind Healing Crystals Explained!". 2019. *The Times Of India*. https://timesofindia.indiatimes.com/life-style/health-fitness/home-remedies/the-science-behind-healing-crystals-explained/articleshow/70482968.cms.

Schlitz, Marilyn. 2005. "Meditation, Prayer And Spiritual Healing: The Evidence". *National Library Of Medicine*. https://www.ncbi.nlm.nih.gov/pmc/articles/PMC3396089/.

Benedetti, Fabrizo, Alessandro Piedimonte, and Elisa Frisaldi. 2018. "How Do Placebos Work?". *National Library Of Medicine*. https://www.ncbi.nlm.nih.gov/pmc/articles/PMC6211282/.

Newman, Tim. 2017. "Placebos: The Power Of The Placebo Effect". *Medicalnewstoday.Com*. https://www.medicalnewstoday.com/articles/306437.

Resnick, Brian. 2017. "The Weird Power Of The Placebo Effect, Explained". *Vox*. https://www.vox.com/science-and-health/2017/7/7/15792188/placebo-effect-explained.

Craen, A J de, P J Roos, A L de Vries, and J Kleijnen. 1996. "Effect Of Colour Of Drugs: Systematic Review Of Perceived Effect Of Drugs And Of Their Effectiveness". *Pubmed.Gov*. https://pubmed.ncbi.nlm.nih.gov/8991013/.

Rybnikova, Olena, and How to Find Rocks Team. 2022. "Rock, Mineral, Or Crystal? What'S The Difference?". *How To Find Rocks*. Accessed September 20. https://howtofindrocks.com/difference-between-rocks-minerals-and-crystals/.

Clark, Donald. 2022. "What Is A Gem? - International Gem Society". *International Gem Society*. Accessed September 20. https://www.gemsociety.org/article/what-is-a-gem/.

"What Is The Difference Between Minerals And Crystals?". 2022. *Geologyin.Com*. Accessed September 20. https://www.geologyin.com/2016/03/what-is-difference-between-minerals-and.html.

Beaudoin, Heather. 2019. "Crystals Vs. Gemstones - What Are The Differences?". *T I N Y B A N D I T*. https://www.tinybandit.com/blog/crystals-vs-gemstones.

Encyclopaedia Britannica, The Editors of. 2020. "Gemstone | Definition, History, Types, & Facts". *Encyclopedia Britannica*. Accessed September 20. https://www.britannica.com/science/gemstone.

Klein, Cornelis, and The Editors of Encyclopaedia Britannica. 2022. "Mineral | Types & Uses". *Encyclopedia Britannica*. https://www.britannica.com/science/mineral-chemical-compound.

Rodrigues, Juliana. 2020. "10 Crystal Shapes And Their Meaning". *New Jersey Digest*. https://thedigestonline.com/blogs/crystal-shapes-and-their-meaning/.

Formtastica, Mme. 2020. "Your Guide To The Top 10 Cut Crystal Shapes - House Of Formlab". *House Of Formlab*. https://houseofformlab.com/your-guide-to-the-top-10-cut-crystal-shapes/.

Wicker, Alycia. 2022. "Why Crystal Shapes Matter + How To Pick The Right One". *Alycia Wicker*. Accessed September 20. https://www.alyciawicker.com/blog/crystal-shapes.

Estrada, Jessica. 2019. "Crystal Shapes Matter—Here'S What They Mean And How To Amplify Their Power". *Well+Good*. https://www.wellandgood.com/crystal-shapes/.

Mael, Michal. 2021. "Crystal Shapes: Meanings And Uses - Michal & Company". *Michal & Company*. https://michalandcompany.com/crystal-shapes-meanings-and-uses/.

"HOW DOES CRYSTAL HEALING WORK & DOES CRYSTAL SIZE MATTER?". 2016. *Crystalangelwings.Com*. https://www.crystalangelwings.com/HOW-DOES-CRYSTAL-HEALING-WORK--&-DOES-CRYSTAL-SIZE-MATTER?/B1.htm.

Lazzerini, Ethan. 2017. "Crystals Does Size Matter For Crystal Healing?". *Ethan Lazzerini*. https://www.ethanlazzerini.com/crystals-does-size-matter/.

Wicker, Alycia. 2022. "Does Crystal Size Matter? Here'S The Truth!". *Alycia Wicker*. Accessed September 20. https://www.alyciaw icker.com/blog/does-crystal-size-matter.

"How Crystals Are Formed". 2022. *Tiny Rituals*. Accessed September 20. https://tinyrituals.co/blogs/tiny-rituals/how-crystals-are-formed.

Shine, Teketa. 2022. "A Beginner's Guide to Clearing, Cleansing, and Charging, Crystals". 2022. *Healthline*. Accessed September 20. https://www.healthline.com/health/how-to-cleanse-crystals.

Young, Olivia. 2021. "How To Cleanse Crystals". *Conscious Items*. https://consciousitems.com/blogs/lifestyle/how-to-cleanse-chakra-stones.

"Cleansing Your Crystals". 2022. *Earth Family Crystals*. Accessed September 20. https://earthfamilycrystals.com/pages/cleansing-your-crystals.

Coughlin, Sara. 2017. "6 Ways To Cleanse Your Healing Crystals". *REFINERY29*. https://www.refinery29.com/en-us/how-to-cleanse-crystals-guide.

Putnam, Rose. 2022. "What Crystals Should You Not Put In Water?". *Crystal Clear Intuition*. https://crystalclearintuition.com/crystals-not-in-water/.

Kahn, Nina. 2018. "How To Cleanse Your Crystals To Maximize Their Healing Vibes". *Bustle*. https://www.bustle.com/life/7-ways-to-cleanse-your-crystals-so-you-can-maximize-on-their-healing-vibes-13244598.

"How To Cleanse Your Crystals And Stones". 2022. *Sacred Gemstone*. Accessed September 20. https://www.sacredgemstone.com/pages/cleansing-crystals-stones.

Young, Olivia. 2021. "How To Cleanse Your Crystals With Selenite". *Conscious Items*. https://consciousitems.com/blogs/prac tice/how-to-cleanse-your-crystals-with-selenite?_pos=1&_sid= 92c37a3ef&_ss=r.

Putnam, Rose. 2022. "Using Rice To Cleanse Negative Energy From Crystals And Why". *Crystal Clear Intuition*. Accessed September 20. https://crystalclearintuition.com/using-rice-to-cleanse-negative-energy-from-crystals-and-why/.

"Crystal Cleansing 101". 2022. *The Hoodwitch*. Accessed September 20. https://www.thehoodwitch.com/blog/2014/9/18/crystal-cleansing-101.

"Cleansing Crystals...". 2022. *Ikigai Holistics*. Accessed September 20. https://ikigaiholistic.co.uk/2021/04/02/cleansing-crystals/.

Delio, Marina. 2021. "How To Cleanse Crystals - 5 Best Ways To Cleanse And Activate Crystals". *Yummy Mummy Kitchen*. https://www.yummymummykitchen.com/2021/07/how-to-cleanse-crystals.html.

"14 Crystals That Can Be In The Sun & Those That Can't". 2022. *Myfaireden: Healing Crystals, Spiritual Jewelry & Metaphysical Shop*. Accessed September 21. https://myfaireden.com/blog/14-crystals-that-can-be-in-the-sun-those-that-cant/?utm_source=rss&utm_medium=rss&utm_campaign=14-crystals-that-can-be-in-the-sun-those-that-cant.

Uilyc, Ceida. 2018. "Which Crystals Can'T Be In The Sun? Find Out Why!". *Atperry's Healing Crystals*. https://shop.atperrys.com/blogs/healing-crystals-blog/which-crystals-can-t-be-in-the-sun-find-out-why

"9 Safe Ways To Purify And Cleanse Crystals – Bliss Crystals". 2022. *Bliss Crystals*. Accessed September 21. https://blisscrystals.com/pages/9-safe-ways-to-cleanse-crystals.

"How To Use And Activate Crystals And Stones". 2021. *Villagerockshop.Com*. https://www.villagerockshop.com/blog/use-activate-crystals-stones/.

"Cleansing Crystals And Stones: Complete Guide (Updated 2022)". 2022. *Shanti Bowl*. Accessed September 23. https://www.shantibowl.com/blogs/blog/the-complete-guide-to-cleansing-crystals-and-stones.

Moscato, Maria. 2022. "7 Convenient Ways To Cleanse Your Healing Crystals". *Yogiapproved ™*. Accessed September 23. https://www.yogiapproved.com/7-convenient-ways-cleanse-healing-crystals/.

"The Powerful Science Behind Setting Intentions - Balance Festival 2023". 2019. *Balance-Festival.Com*. https://www.balance-festival.

com/Journal/February-2019/The-Powerful-Science-Behind-Setting-Intentions.

"The Biology Of Intention-Setting: Our Body'S Response To Activating The Mind". 2022. *Thriveglobal.Com*. Accessed September 23. https://thriveglobal.com/stories/the-biology-of-intention-setting-our-bodys-response-to-activating-the-mind/.

Kahn, Nina. 2021. "How To Use Crystals To Manifest Your Desires". *Bustle*. https://www.bustle.com/life/how-to-charge-crystals-set-your-intentions-when-you-meditate-with-them-18788303.

Mehdi, Shirin. 2022. "Secrets Of Deep Meditation – How To Meditate Deeply". *STYLECRAZE*. https://www.stylecraze.com/articles/deep-meditation-procedure-and-techniques/.

Meditation, About. 2012. "How To Enter Into A Meditative State". *About Meditation*. https://aboutmeditation.com/how-to-meditate-2/.

Moon, Hibiscus. 2022. "How To Program A Crystal". *Hibiscus Moon Crystal Academy*. Accessed September 23. https://hibiscusmooncrystalacademy.com/how-to-program-a-crystal/.

Lazzerini, Ethan. 2016. "How To Program Crystals For Beginners". *Ethan Lazzerini*. https://www.ethanlazzerini.com/how-to-program-crystals/.

Regan, Sarah. 2021. "10 Types Of Healing Crystals For Beginners & How To Use Each | Mindbodygreen". *Mindbodygreen.Com*. https://www.mindbodygreen.com/articles/types-of-crystals.

Stokes, Victoria. 2021. "Love, Health, Success, Or Wealth? How To Use Crystals To Manifest Your Desires". *Healthline*. https://www.healthline.com/health/crystals-for-manifestation.

"What Crystals Cannot Be Cleansed In Water? - Crystal Healing Ritual". 2022. *Crystal Healing Ritual*. https://www.crystalhealingritual.com/what-crystals-cannot-be-cleansed-in-water/.

"How To Cleanse Celestite? 4 Safe Tools | Crystals And Joy". 2022. *Crystals And Joy*. Accessed September 24. https://crystalsandjoy.com/how-to-cleanse-celestite/.

"How To Cleanse Chrysocolla? Answered | Crystals And Joy". 2022. *Crystals And Joy*. Accessed September 24. https://crystalsandjoy.com/how-to-cleanse-chrysocolla/.

"How To Cleanse Fluorite? Answered. | Crystals And Joy". 2022. *Crystals And Joy*. Accessed September 24. https://crystalsandjoy.com/how-to-cleanse-fluorite/.

"How To Cleanse Aventurine: 5 Effective Methods Explained | Calming Cosmos". 2022. *Calming Cosmos*. Accessed September 24. https://calmingcosmos.com/how-to-cleanse-aventurine-5-effective-methods-explained/.

"Can Aventurine Go In Water? (ANSWER With Simple Explanation) - Yes Dirt". 2022. *Yes Dirt*. Accessed September 24. https://yesdirt.com/can-aventurine-go-in-water/.

"Can Labradorite Get Wet? - Yes Dirt". 2022. *Yes Dirt*. Accessed September 24. https://yesdirt.com/can-labradorite-get-wet/.

Hayo, Eran. 2021. "Can Lapis Lazuli Go In Water? My Honest, Tested Answer". *Jewels Advisor*. https://jewelsadvisor.com/can-lapis-lazuli-go-in-water/.

"Which Crystals Fade In The Sun? (And How To Protect Them) - Minerals Geek". 2020. *Minerals Geek*. https://www.mineralsgeek.com/which-crystals-fade-in-the-sun-and-how-to-protect-them/.

Dee, Mystic. 2022. "Can MALACHITE Go In Water? Read This Before You Dip It In Water.". *You Are My Magic*. Accessed September 24. https://youaremymagic.com/can-malachite-go-in-water/.

"Can Moonstone Go In Water? (ANSWERED) - Yes Dirt". 2022. *Yes Dirt*. Accessed September 24. https://yesdirt.com/can-moonstone-go-in-water/.

Putnam, Rose. 2022. "Can Pyrite Get Wet? Here Are Better Ways To Cleanse It". *Crystal Clear Intuition*. Accessed September 24. https://crystalclearintuition.com/can-pyrite-get-wet/.

Hayo, Eran. 2021. "Can Red Jasper Go In Water? My Honest, Tested Answer". *Jewels Advisor*. https://jewelsadvisor.com/can-red-jasper-go-in-water/.

Hayo, Eran. 2021. "Can Rhodonite Go In Water? My Honest, Tested

Answer". *Jewels Advisor*. https://jewelsadvisor.com/can-rhodonite-go-in-water/.

"Does Selenite Dissolve In Water? (Read This Before You Clean Your Crystal) - Yes Dirt". 2022. *Yes Dirt*. Accessed September 24. https://yesdirt.com/does-selenite-dissolve-in-water/.

Young, Olivia. 2020. "Sodalite: How To Use Its Energy To Balance Mind, Body, And Soul". *Conscious Items*. https://consciousitems.com/blogs/crystal-guides/sodalite.

Young, Olivia. 2022. "Water Safe Crystals: What Crystals Can And Cannot Go In Water". *Conscious Items*. https://consciousitems.com/blogs/practice/water-crystals-what-crystals-can-go-in-water.

"Mycrystals.Com - Healing Crystals". 2022. *Mycrystals.Com*. Accessed September 24. https://www.mycrystals.com/.

"Discover More. Feel Inspired. Make Forever Memories.". 2022. *Truly Experiences Blog*. Accessed September 24. https://trulyexperiences.com/blog/.

"Crystal Encyclopedia - Crystal Vaults". 2022. *Crystalvaults.Com*. Accessed September 24. https://www.crystalvaults.com/crystal-encyclopedia/.

"7 Best Crystals For Depression - Beadnova". 2022. *Beadnova*. Accessed September 24. https://www.beadnova.com/blog/22082/7-best-crystals-for-depression.

"Top 10 Crystals & Stones Good For Depression | Village Rock Shop". 2020. *Villagerockshop.Com*. https://www.villagerockshop.com/blog/crystals-stones-for-depression/.

"Crystals For Depression: 16 Stones To Clear The Mind". 2022. *Tiny Rituals*. Accessed September 24. https://tinyrituals.co/blogs/tiny-rituals/crystals-for-depression-16-stones-to-clear-the-mind.

"Crystals For Sadness: How To Shift From Sadness To Happiness". 2022. *Energy Muse*. Accessed September 24. https://energymuse.com/blogs/guides/crystals-for-sadness.

Davis, Faith. 2022. "10 Crystals For Depression: Mood-Enhancing Stones To Restore Yourself". *Cosmic Cuts*. Accessed September 24. https://cosmiccuts.com/en-ca/blogs/healing-stones-blog/crystals-for-depression.

"13 Best Crystals For Depression (Updated 2022)". 2022. *Healing Crystals Co.*. Accessed September 24. https://www.healingcrystalsco. com/blogs/blog/13-best-crystals-for-depression.

Guling, Elizabeth. 2020. "Feeling Blue? Astrologers Are Using These 6 Crystals To Combat Bad Moods". *REFINERY29*. https://www.refin ery29.com/en-us/healing-crystals-depression.

"Healing Crystals For Depression | Best Stones For Anxiety". 2022. *Crystals And Stones*. Accessed September 24. https://www.crys talsandstones.com/crystals-for-depression-and-anxiety.

Houston, Diana. 2022. "Crystals For Depression – The Complete Guide". *Crystalsandjewelry.Com*. Accessed September 24. https:// meanings.crystalsandjewelry.com/crystals-self-harm-depression/.

"Crystals For Happiness - Beadnova". 2022. *Beadnova*. Accessed September 24. https://www.beadnova.com/blog/24249/crystals-for-happiness.

Davis, Faith. 2022. "Happiness Crystals: The 10 Best Crystals For Happiness, Joy & Positivi". *Cosmic Cuts*. Accessed September 24. https://cosmiccuts.com/blogs/healing-stones-blog/happiness-crys tals-the-10-best-crystals-for-happiness-joy-positivity.

Oakes, Liz. 2022. "Top 30 Crystals For Happiness Meanings & Properties & Powers". *Healingcrystalsforyou.Com*. Accessed September 24. https://www.healing-crystals-for-you.com/crystals-for-happi ness.html.

"20 Best Crystals For Happiness And Positive Energy". 2022. *Healing Crystals Co.*. Accessed September 24. https://www.healingcrys talsco.com/blogs/blog/crystals-for-happiness-and-positive-energy.

"Crystals For Happiness: How To Shift From Darkness To Light". 2022. *Energy Muse*. Accessed September 25. https://energymuse. com/blogs/crystals/crystals-for-happiness-positivity.

"The Best Crystals & Gemstones For More Joy & Happiness". 2022. *BEADAGE Healing Jewelry & Gems*. Accessed September 25. https://beadage.net/gemstones/uses/joy/.

"15 Best Crystals To Bring Happiness And Joy To Your Life". 2022. *Tiny Rituals*. Accessed September 25. https://tinyrituals.co/blogs/tiny-rituals/15-best-crystals-to-bring-happiness-and-joy-to-your-life.

Crawford, Charles. 2022. "10 Crystals For Positive Energy & Happiness". *Lifehack*. Accessed September 25. https://www.lifehack.org/469922/10-crystals-for-positive-energy-happiness.

"8 Crystals For Calming Yourself From Anxiety And Anger - Beadnova". 2022. *Beadnova*. Accessed September 25. https://www.beadnova.com/blog/14714/crystals-for-calming-anger.

"24 Crystals That Can Relieve Anger, Frustration, & Stress". 2022. *Tiny Rituals*. Accessed September 25. https://tinyrituals.co/blogs/tiny-rituals/crystals-for-anger.

"Top 5 Crystals For Anger And Stress | Village Rock Shop". 2020. *Villagerockshop.Com*. https://www.villagerockshop.com/blog/crystals-for-anger-and-stress/.

Davis, Faith. 2022. "Crystals For Anger: Diffuse Frustration, Irritability & Temper". *Cosmic Cuts*. Accessed September 25. https://cosmiccuts.com/en-ca/blogs/healing-stones-blog/crystals-for-anger.

Young, Olivia. 2022. "The Best Crystals To Help With Anger Management". *Conscious Items*. https://consciousitems.com/blogs/practice/the-best-crystals-to-help-with-anger-management.

Ancillette, Mary. 2022. "9 Healing Crystals For Anger And Irritability". *Angel Grotto*. https://angelgrotto.com/crystals-stones/anger/.

"9 Powerful Crystals To Keep Your Anger In Check". 2022. *Jaime Pfeffer*. Accessed September 25. https://jaimepfeffer.com/2018/12/03/9-powerful-crystals-to-keep-your-anger-in-check/.

"12 Stones And Crystals To Reduce Anger And Frustration | Japa Mala Beads". 2022. *Japa Mala Beads*. Accessed September 25. https://japamalabeads.com/stones-crystals-for-anger%E2%80%A8/.

"Crystals For Anger: How To Shift From Anger To Love". 2022. *Energy Muse*. Accessed September 25. https://energymuse.com/blogs/guides/crystals-for-anger.

Davis, Faith. 2022. "13 Crystals For Fear And Anxiety & How To Use Them". *Cosmic Cuts*. Accessed September 25. https://cosmiccuts.com/blogs/healing-stones-blog/crystals-for-fear.

Kahn, Nina. 2019. "The 5 Best Crystals To Keep Around For Stress

Relief". *Bustle.* https://www.bustle.com/p/5-crystals-for-stress-relief-how-to-use-them-to-feel-more-zen-18799729.

Delio, Marina. 2021. "Crystals For Anxiety - 5 Best Crystals For Anxiety And Stress". *Yummy Mummy Kitchen.* https://www.yummy mummykitchen.com/2021/07/crystals-for-anxiety.html.

Chee, Chermaine. 2021. "10 Best Crystals For Anxiety, Stress & Healing". *Truly Experiences Blog.* https://trulyexperiences.com/blog/crys tals-for-anxiety-stress-healing/.

"6 Best Healing Crystals For Anxiety & Stress". 2020. *RETREALM.* https://retrealm.com/blogs/living/6-best-healing-crystals-for-anxi ety-stress.

"20 Healing Crystals For Anxiety & Stress". 2022. *Tiny Rituals.* Accessed September 25. https://tinyrituals.co/blogs/tiny-rituals/crystals-for-anxiety.

"8 Crystals & Stones To Relieve Stress & Anxiety | Village Rock Shop". 2018. *Villagerockshop.Com.* https://www.villagerockshop.com/blog/ eight-healing-stones-to-relieve-stress-and-anxiety/.

"11 Best Crystals That Can Help With Anxiety". 2022. *Upskillist Blog.* Accessed September 25. https://blog.upskillist.com/best-healing-crystals-for-anxiety/.

Roberts, Taylor. 2021. "24 Crystals For Calming Stress And Anxiety". *Sarah Scoop.* https://sarahscoop.com/24-crystals-for-calm ing-stress-and-anxiety/.

Gulino, Elizabeth. 2020. "5 Calming Crystals To Melt Away Anxiety". *REFINERY29.* https://www.refinery29.com/en-ca/crys tals-for-anxiety.

"15 Best Crystals For Anxiety (Updated 2022)". 2022. *Healing Crystals Co..* https://www.healingcrystalsco.com/blogs/blog/15-best-crys tals-for-anxiety.

"7 Best Crystals For Better Sleep - Beadnova". 2022. *Beadnova.* Accessed September 25. https://www.beadnova.com/blog/14520/7-best-crystals-for-better-sleep.

"5 Crystals To Sleep With". 2019. *The Goodnight Co..* https://www. thegoodnightco.com.au/blogs/the-journal/5-crystals-to-sleep-with.

Young, Olivia. 2022. "14 Calming Crystals For Sleep And How To Use Them For A Night Rest". *Conscious Items*. https://consciousitems.com/blogs/practice/best-crystals-for-sleep-and-dreams.

Stokes, Victoria. 2021. "Crystals For Sleep: Catch More ZZZ'S With These Healing Stones". *Healthline*. https://www.healthline.com/health/sleep/crystals-for-sleep.

Chee, Chermaine. 2021. "10 Best Calming Crystals For Sleep & Insomnia". *Truly Experiences Blog*. https://trulyexperiences.com/blog/crystals-for-sleep/.

Sherpa, Sleep. 2022. "Best Crystals For Sleep - Expert Picks". *Sleep Sherpa*. https://sleepsherpa.com/best-crystals-for-sleep/.

"21 Best Crystals For Sleep, Insomnia And Dreams (Updated 2022)". 2022. *Healing Crystals Co.*. https://www.healingcrystalsco.com/blogs/blog/crystals-for-sleep-insomnia-and-dreams.

Roberts, Taylor. 2021. "25 Best Crystals For Sleep". *Sarah Scoop*. https://sarahscoop.com/25-best-crystals-for-sleep/.

"8 Types Of Crystals To Use For Sleep: Sleep Better With Crystals (2022 Updated)". 2022. *Terry Cralle*. https://www.terrycralle.com/crystals-for-sleep/.

"The 3 Healing Crystals That You Need For Your Bedroom". 2022. *Aulitfinelinens.Com*. Accessed September 25. https://www.aulitfinelinens.com/blogs/betweenthesheets/the-3-healing-crystals-that-you-need-for-your-bedroom.

Alnuweiri, Tamim. 2018. "The 5 Best Crystals For Better Sleep | Well+Good". *Well+Good*. https://www.wellandgood.com/crystals-for-sleep/.

Oakes, Jodies. 2020. "Crystals For Sleep: 10 Stones To Get You Into REM". *Tiny Rituals*. https://tinyrituals.co/blogs/tiny-rituals/crystals-for-sleep-10-stones-to-get-you-into-rem.

"14 Crystals For Headaches & Migraines – Find Relief!". 2022. *Tiny Rituals*. Accessed September 25. https://tinyrituals.co/blogs/tiny-rituals/14-crystals-for-headaches-migraines-find-relief.

Satin, Sheila, and Nicole McCray. 2021. "7 Powerful Crystals For Headaches". *Satin Crystals*. https://satincrystals.com/blogs/news/7-powerful-crystals-for-headaches.

Houston, Diana. 2022. "Crystals For Headaches – The Complete Guide". *Crystalsandjewelry.Com*. Accessed September 25. https://meanings.crystalsandjewelry.com/crystals-for-headaches/.

"Crystals For Headaches & Pain Relief". 2022. *Energy Muse*. Accessed September 25. https://energymuse.com/blogs/crystals/crystals-for-headaches.

"12 Healing Crystals For Migraines And Headaches". 2022. *Crystal Healing Ritual*. https://www.crystalhealingritual.com/crystals-for-migraines/.

Davis, Faith. 2022. "12 Best Crystals For Headaches, Migraines & Sinus Pressure". *Cosmic Cuts*. Accessed September 25. https://cosmiccuts.com/en-ca/blogs/healing-stones-blog/crystals-for-headaches.

"Crystals For Headache & Migraine Relief". 2020. *808 Wellness Spa, Maui*. https://808wellness.com/crystals-for-headache-migraine-relief/.

"The Best Gemstones And Crystals For A Healthy Pregnancy + Childbirth". 2022. *Injewels Healing Jewelry*. Accessed September 25. https://injewels.net/blogs/news/78765636-gemstones-and-crystals-for-a-healthy-pregnancy-childbirth.

Julian-Arndt, Yvette. 2022. "Crystals For Pregnancy, Birth And Postpartum - Peninsula Kids". *Peninsula Kids*. Accessed September 25. http://peninsulakids.com.au/crystals-for-pregnancy-birth-and-postpartum/.

Stones, Samata. 2018. "The Best Stones For Pregnancy And Motherhood". *Samata Stones*. https://samatastones.com/blogs/blog/the-best-stones-for-pregnancy-and-motherhood.

"19 Top Crystals For Fertility And Pregnancy". 2022. *Healing Crystals Co.*. Accessed September 25. https://www.healingcrystalsco.com/blogs/blog/crystals-for-fertility-and-pregnancy.

Grassullo, Stephanie. 2020. "Best Healing Crystals For Postpartum Moms". *The BUMP*. https://www.thebump.com/a/healing-crystals-new-moms.

Houston, Diana. 2022. "Crystals For Pregnancy – The Complete Guide". *Crystalsandjewelry.Com*. Accessed September 25. https://meanings.crystalsandjewelry.com/crystals-pregnancy-complete-guide/.

"10 Powerful Crystals For Safe Pregnancy, Birth And Motherhood". 2022. *Tiny Rituals*. Accessed September 25. https://tinyrituals.co/blogs/tiny-rituals/10-powerful-crystals-for-safe-pregnancy-birth-and-motherhood.

"Best Crystals For Protection | Protection Stones - Moonmagic – Moon Magic". 2021. *Shop.Moonmagic.Com*. https://shop.moonmagic.com/blogs/news/stones-and-crystals-for-protection?select_store=1.

McKinstry, Katiee. 2021. "The 5 Best Crystals For Protection". *Yoga Journal*. https://www.yogajournal.com/lifestyle/crystals-for-protection/.

Chee, Chermaine. 2021. "6 Of The Best Crystals For Protection: Meaning & How To Use". *Truly Experiences Blog*. https://trulyexperiences.com/blog/crystals-for-protection/.

Stardust, Lisa. 2022. "The Crystals That'Ll Keep ~Bad Vibes~ Away, Based On Your Zodiac Sign". *Cosmopolitan*. https://www.cosmopolitan.com/lifestyle/g31082493/best-crystals-for-protection-zodiac-sign/.

Young, Olivia. 2022. "What Are The Top 10 Crystals For Protection And How Do You Use Them?". *Conscious Items*. https://consciousitems.com/blogs/practice/top-10-crystals-for-protection.

"Best Crystals For Protection - The Complete Guide (2021)". 2022. *Mycrystals.Com*. https://www.mycrystals.com/use/best-crystals-for-protection.

Hui, Vanessa. 2021. "5 Powerful Crystals For Battling Toxic People And Negative Energy — Hashtag Legend". *Hashtag Legend*. https://hashtaglegend.com/beauty/wellness/5-powerful-crystals-for-battling-toxic-people-and-negative-energy/.

Gulino, Elizabeth. 2020. "5 Happy Crystals That Ward Off Negative Energy". *REFINERY29*. https://www.refinery29.com/en-us/crystals-for-protection.

"9 Best Crystals For Protection - Beadnova". 2022. *Beadnova*. Accessed September 25. https://www.beadnova.com/blog/13554/best-crystals-for-protection.

Skon, Julie. 2021. "6 Crystals To Protect Yourself From Toxic People & Negative Energy". *Mindbodygreen*. https://www.mindbodygreen.com/articles/crystals-for-protection.

Askinosie, Heather. 2019. "The Best Crystals For Love, Creativity & Protection From A Healer | Mindbodygreen". *Mindbodygreen.Com*. https://www.mindbodygreen.com/articles/these-are-the-best-crystals-for-love-creativity-and-protection.

"7 Best Crystals To Attract Love And Romance - Beadnova". 2022. *Beadnova*. Accessed September 25. https://www.beadnova.com/blog/13500/crystals-to-attract-love-and-romance.

"17 Crystals For Love: Manifest The Love Life Of Your Dreams". 2022. *Tiny Rituals*. Accessed September 25. https://tinyrituals.co/blogs/tiny-rituals/8-gemstones-that-will-manifest-the-love-life-of-your-dreams.

Parpworth-Reynolds, Chloe. 2022. "Crystals For Manifesting Love And Romance (The 17 Best Ones)". *Subconscious Servant*. https://subconsciousservant.com/manifesting-love-and-romance-crystals/.

Kahn, Nina. 2020. "You'll Want To Use These 5 Crystals For Positive Vibes On Valentine's Day". *Bustle*. https://www.bustle.com/p/5-crystals-for-valentines-day-2020-thatll-manifest-love-positive-vibes-18796090.

Mildon, Emma. 2021. "How To Use Crystals To Attract Your Soul Mate". *Mindbodygreen*. https://www.mindbodygreen.com/articles/crystals-to-attract-your-soul-mate.

"GEMSTONES FOR LOVE: Crystals That Support & Attract Romance 💚". 2022. *Mexicali Blues*. https://www.mexicaliblues.com/blogs/our-stories-mexicali-blues-blog/gemstones-for-love-crystals-that-support-attract-romance.

Stokes, Victoria. 2021. "Love, Health, Success, Or Wealth? How To Use Crystals To Manifest Your Desires". *Healthline*. https://www.healthline.com/health/crystals-for-manifestation.

"7 Best Crystals To Bring Luck And Wealth & Guide On How To Place Them - Beadnova". 2022. *Beadnova*. Accessed September 25. https://www.beadnova.com/blog/14653/7-best-crystals-to-bring-luck-and-wealth-guide-on-how-to-place-them.

"9 Best Crystals To Attract Money And Bring Wealth - Beadnova". 2022. *Beadnova*. Accessed September 25. https://www.beadnova.com/blog/13517/best-crystals-to-attract-money-and-bring-wealth.

Kellner, Lindsay. 2020. "Want To Manifest More Money? Make Sure You Have The Right Crystals". *Mindbodygreen*. https://www.mindbodygreen.com/articles/crystals-to-help-raise-your-money-vibes.

"7 Powerful Crystals To Attract Money | The Manifestation Collective". 2020. *The Manifestation Collective | Manifestation Coaching In The UK*. https://themanifestationcollective.co/crystals-to-attract-money/.

Stokes, Jodie. 2020. "Crystals For Money: 17 Stones To Create True Prosperity". *Tiny Rituals*. https://tinyrituals.co/blogs/tiny-rituals/crystals-for-money-17-stones-to-create-true-prosperity.

Chee, Chermaine. 2021. "10 Best Crystals For Money: Stones To Attract Wealth & Prosperity". *Truly Experiences Blog*. https://trulyexperiences.com/blog/crystals-for-money/.

Young, Olivia. 2022. "Best Crystals For Money, Prosperity, And Abundance (& How To Use Them)". *Conscious Items*. https://consciousitems.com/blogs/practice/best-crystals-for-money-wealth-and-abundance.

Zarate, Arlette. 2021. "15 Crystals For Manifesting Money And Prosperity". *Sarah Scoop*. https://sarahscoop.com/15-crystals-for-manifesting-money-and-prosperity/.

"10 Best Powerful Crystals For Health - Beadnova". 2022. *Beadnova*. Accessed September 25. https://www.beadnova.com/blog/13510/best-crystals-for-health.

Caro, Gina. 2022. "11 Crystals For Better Health And Wellbeing". *Gypsy Soul*. Accessed September 25. https://www.gypsysoul.co.uk/11-crystals-for-better-health-and-wellbeing-3/.

"15 Crystals For Good Health & Wellness". 2022. *Tiny Rituals*. Accessed September 25. https://tinyrituals.co/blogs/tiny-rituals/crystals-for-health.

Wolf, Jenna. 2017. "Gemstones For Health And Happiness". *Tennessean.Com*. https://www.tennessean.com/story/life/entertainment/12th/2017/03/08/gemstones-health-and-happiness/98864266/.

Brown, Devi. 2017. "5 Crystals To Tap For Self-Care And Optimal Health". *Yoga Journal*. https://www.yogajournal.com/yoga-101/5-crystals-to-tap-for-self-care-and-optimal-health/.

"Crystals For Creativity That Enhance Your Creative - Beadnova". 2022. *Beadnova*. Accessed September 25. https://www.beadnova.com/blog/24260/crystals-for-creativity.

Hall, Judy. 2016. "10 Crystals To Tap For Creativity And Inspiration". *Yoga Journal*. https://www.yogajournal.com/yoga-101/10-crystals-tap-creativity-inspiration/.

"12 Powerful Crystals For Creativity - Enhance Your Creative Energy". 2022. *Tiny Rituals*. Accessed September 25. https://tinyrituals.co/blogs/tiny-rituals/12-powerful-crystals-for-creativity-enhance-your-creative-energy.

"Best Crystals For Creativity - The Complete Guide (2021)". 2022. *Mycrystals.Com*. Accessed September 25. https://www.mycrystals.com/use/best-crystals-for-creativity.

Davis, Faith. 2022. "Top 12 Crystals For Creativity: Get Unstuck & Boost Your Imagination". *Cosmic Cuts*. Accessed September 25. https://cosmiccuts.com/en-ca/blogs/healing-stones-blog/crystals-for-creativity.

Parpworth-Reynolds, Chloe. 2022. "11 Of The BEST Crystals To Help Enhance Your Creativity". *Subconscious Servant*. https://subconsciousservant.com/crystals-for-creativity/.

Houston, Diana. 2022. "Crystals For Creativity – The Complete Guide". *Crystalsandjewelry.Com*. Accessed September 25. https://meanings.crystalsandjewelry.com/crystals-creativity-guide/.

Ancillette, Mary. 2022. "9 Powerful Gems And Crystals For Boosting Creativity". *Angel Grotto*. https://angelgrotto.com/crystals-stones/creativity/.

Cohen, Jennifer. 2019. "9 Crystals That Increase Focus And Productivity". *Forbes.* https://www.forbes.com/sites/jennifercohen/2019/09/04/9-crystals-that-increase-focus-and-productivity/?sh=79419e535424.

Twist, Divine. 2022. "10 Amazing Crystals For Focus + Concentration". *Divine Twist.* https://www.divinetwist.com/crystals-for-focus/.

"15 Crystals For Motivation: Change Your Life!". 2022. *Tiny Rituals.* Accessed September 25. https://tinyrituals.co/blogs/tiny-rituals/15-crystals-for-motivation-change-your-life.

"Best Crystals For Focus - The Complete Guide (2021)". 2022. *Mycrystals.Com.* Accessed September 25. https://www.mycrystals.com/use/best-crystals-for-focus.

Harrison, Michael. 2022. "10 Healing Crystals For Concentration And Focus". *Cosmic Cuts.* Accessed September 25. https://cosmiccuts.com/blogs/healing-stones-blog/healing-crystals-for-concentration-and-focus.

"Crystals And Stones For Focus, Productivity, Motivation And Manifestation!". 2020. *Belle Amorette | Lunar Girl Living.* https://www.belleamorette.com/crystals-and-stones-to-help-with-productivity-motivation-and-manifestation/.

"Best Crystals To Promote Creativity, Focus & Concentration | Village Rock Shop". 2020. *Villagerockshop.Com.* https://www.villagerockshop.com/blog/best-crystals-to-promote-creativity-focus-concentration/.

"17 Best Crystals For Motivation, Productivity, Creativity, And Focus". 2021. *Shutter OWL Photography.* https://www.shutterowlphotography.com/crystals-for-motivation-productivity-creativity-and-focus/.

Young, Olivia. 2021. "Crystals For Focus And Motivation: The 8 Best Crystals For Clarity". *Conscious Items.* https://consciousitems.com/blogs/practice/crystals-for-focus-and-motivation.

Cornford-Matheson, Alison. 2022. "Welcome 2022 With 10 Gemstones For New Beginnings". *Fierce Lynx Designs.* https://fiercelynxdesigns.com/blogs/articles/welcome-2021-with-10-gemstones-for-new-beginnings.

Ancillette, Mary. 2022. "9 Healing Crystals For New Beginnings And Fresh Starts". *Angel Grotto.* https://angelgrotto.com/crystals-stones/new-beginnings/.

"12 Life Changing Crystals For New Beginnings - Crystal Healing Ritual". 2022. *Crystal Healing Ritual.* https://www.crystalhealingritual.com/crystals-for-new-beginnings/.

"Renewal And New Beginnings: Gemstones For Channeling Spring's Energy.". 2019. *Lovepray Jewelry.* https://www.loveprayjewelry.com/blogs/news/gemstones-for-renewal-and-new-beginnings.

"Best Crystals For Change And New Beginnings". 2022. *Crystals And Stones.* Accessed September 25. https://www.crystalsandstones.com/new-beginnings.

"Gemstones For A New Beginning - 10 Stones To Drive A Fresh Start". 2022. *Gemselect.Com.* Accessed September 25. https://www.gemselect.com/other-info/gems-for-new-beginnings.php.

Young, Olivia. 2020. "The Top 5 Crystals For New Beginnings". *Conscious Items.* https://consciousitems.com/blogs/lifestyle/top-5-crystals-for-new-beginnings-and-how-to-use-them-to-set-intentions.

Hui, Vanessa. 2021. "5 Crystals For Summoning Courage And Confidence — Hashtag Legend". *Hashtag Legend.* https://hashtaglegend.com/beauty/wellness/5-crystals-for-summoning-courage-and-confidence/.

Lorenz, Taylor. 2022. "11 Best Crystals For Confidence & Courage To Be You". *Taylor's Tracks.* https://www.taylorstracks.com/best-crystals-for-confidence/.

"Crystals For Confidence & Courage". 2022. *BEADAGE Healing Jewelry & Gems.* Accessed September 25. https://beadage.net/gemstones/uses/confidence/.

"8 Best Crystals For Confidence - Boost Your Self Confidence". 2022. *Tiny Rituals.* Accessed September 25. https://tinyrituals.co/blogs/tiny-rituals/8-best-crystals-for-confidence-boost-your-self-confidence.

Ancillette, Mary. 2022. "9 Best Crystals And Gemstones For

Courage". *Angel Grotto.* https://angelgrotto.com/crystals-stones/courage/.

"Crystals For Confidence: The Best Gems For Believing In Yourself". 2019. *Crystals For Humanity.* https://gem-water.com/blogs/crystals-for-humanity-blog/crystals-for-confidence-the-best-gems-for-believing-in-yourself.

Davis, Faith. 2022. "9 Best Crystals For Courage: Don'T Let Anything Stop You". *Cosmic Cuts.* Accessed September 25. https://cosmiccuts.com/en-ca/blogs/healing-stones-blog/best-crystals-for-courage.

"10 Best Crystals For Courage And Confidence - Beadnova". 2022. *Beadnova.* Accessed September 25. https://www.beadnova.com/blog/14656/best-crystals-for-courage.

"Chakras & Crystals: The Ultimate Guide". 2022. *Tiny Rituals.* Accessed September 25. https://tinyrituals.co/blogs/tiny-rituals/chakra-crystals.

Tracy, Jessica. 2020. "Chakra Stones Meanings | 7 Chakras Crystals Chart". *7 Chakra Store.* https://7chakrastore.com/blogs/news/chakra-stones.

"The Best Ethical Chakra Crystals". 2021. *Be My Travel Muse.* https://www.bemytravelmuse.com/chakra-crystals/.

Lee, Precious, and Chioma Nnadi. 2021. "Precious Lee's Guide to Chakra Healing". *Vogue.* https://www.vogue.com/article/precious-lee-chakra-guide.

"The Seven Chakras: Meaning, Gemstones & Crystals". 2022. *Manipura Malas.* Accessed September 25. https://manipuramala.com/pages/chakras.

Kahn, Nina. 2018. "11 Unexpected Ways To Use Crystals For Healing". *Bustle.* https://www.bustle.com/p/11-unexpected-ways-to-use-crystals-for-healing-instead-of-just-for-decoration-13253677.

Butterworth, Lisa. 2019. "The Yogi's Ultimate Crystal Ritual Guide". *Yoga Journal.* https://www.yogajournal.com/yoga-101/crystal-rituals/.

Coxon, Sarah. 2017. "The 3 Crystals Every Yogi Should Have (And

Exactly How To Use 'Em)". *Mindbodygreen.Com.* https://www.mind
bodygreen.com/articles/3-crystals-perfect-for-yogis.

Stokes, Victoria. 2020. "How To Meditate With Crystals: Getting
Started, Methods, And Types". *Healthline.* https://www.healthline.
com/health/meditate-with-crystals.

"How To Use Crystals + How To Cleanse Your Crystals — The Well-
ness Nest | Melbourne Myotherapist". 2020. *The Wellness Nest |
Melbourne Myotherapist.* https://www.thewellnessnest.com.au/blog/
how-to-use-crystals.

"Crystals As High Vibe Decor". 2021. *Crystal Visions.* https://crystalvi
sions.net.au/blogs/an-introduction-to-crystal-grids/crystals-as-
high-vibe-decor-in-the-home-or-office.

"12 Crystals For The Bedroom & Where To Place Them". 2022. *Tiny
Rituals.* Accessed September 25. https://tinyrituals.co/blogs/tiny-
rituals/crystals-for-bedroom.

"Crystals For Your Home: Turn It Into A High-Vibe Crystal Heaven".
2022. *Energy Muse.* Accessed September 25. https://energymuse.
com/blogs/guides/crystals-for-your-home.

Humes, Jessica. 2021. "Crystals For Bathroom: Cleanse And Energise
With These Crystals". *Humeshed.* https://humeshed.com/spiritual/
crystals-for-bathroom/.

"Crystals For The Kitchen". 2022. *Crystal Cove.* Accessed September 25.
https://www.crystalcove.com.au/collections/crystals-for-the-
kitchen.

"Crystals To Keep In Your Office | Village Rock Shop". 2021. *Village-
rockshop.Com.* https://www.villagerockshop.com/blog/crystals-
office/.

Davis, Faith. 2022. "Best Crystals For Your Car, Plus Why & How To
Use Them". *Cosmic Cuts.* Accessed September 25. https://cosmic
cuts.com/en-ca/blogs/healing-stones-blog/crystals-for-your-car.

Young, Olivia. 2021. "Crystals For Car Protection: 7 Best Crystals To
Keep In Your Car". *Conscious Items.* https://consciousitems.com/
blogs/practice/crystals-to-keep-in-your-car.

"8 Best Crystals To Keep In Car For Protection While Driving - Beadnova". 2022. *Beadnova*. Accessed September 25. https://www.bead nova.com/blog/23274/crystals-for-car-protection.

"Crystals To Keep In Your Car | Village Rock Shop". 2021. *Villagerock-shop.Com*. https://www.villagerockshop.com/blog/crystals-car/.

"Manifesting With Crystals-The Best Crystals For Manifesting". 2022. *Mystic Crystal Imports*. Accessed September 25. https://mystic crystalimports.com/pages/manifesting-with-crystals.

Young, Olivia. 2022. "12 Best Crystals For Manifesting Love, Abundance, And Personal Power". *Conscious Items*. https:// consciousitems.com/blogs/practice/best-crystals-for-manifesting.

Askinosie, Heather. 2022. "SACRED TOOLS FOR CREATING A SACRED SPACE ANYWHERE". *TEACH.YOGA*. https://teach.yoga/ sacred-tools-for-creating-a-sacred-space-anywhere/.

Montell, Amanda. 2020. "How To Cast A Happiness Spell On Yourself, According To A Real-Life Witch". *Byrdie*. https://www.byrdie.com/ spell-for-happiness.

Young, Olivia. 2020. "Crystal Rituals: The Ultimate Guide". *Conscious Items*. https://consciousitems.com/blogs/practice/crystal-rituals-the-ultimate-guide.

Askinosie, Heather. 2022. "Sacred Space: Why You Need It + How To Create One In Your Home". *Energy Muse*. Accessed September 26. https://energymuse.com/blogs/guides/create-sacred-space-medita tion.

Kuruvilla, Carol. 2016. "How To Create A Sacred Space In Your Home". *Huffpost UK*. https://www.huffpost.com/entry/how-to-create-a-sacred-space-in-your-home _n_56d72b12e4b03260bf78e917.

"HOW TO CREATE A CRYSTAL ALTAR - Earth Crystals". 2019. *Earth Crystals*. https://www.earthcrystals.com.au/create-crystal-altar/.

Young, Olivia. 2022. "How To Set Up Your Meditation Crystal Altar". *Conscious Items*. https://consciousitems.com/blogs/practice/ how-to-set-up-your-meditation-crystal-altar.

"Create A Crystal Altar To Hold The Space For Your Intention". 2022. *Energy Muse*. Accessed September 26. https://energymuse. com/blogs/practices/crystal-altar.

Askinosie, Heather. 2022. "How To Make Your Own Crystal Grid". *Energy Muse*. Accessed September 26. https://energymuse.com/blogs/crystals/crystal-grids.

"Crystal Grids: Complete Guide (Updated 2022)". 2022. *Healing Crystals Co.*. https://www.healingcrystalsco.com/blogs/blog/crystal-grids-complete-guide.

NOTES

1. WITCHCRAFT: THE PAST, PRESENT, AND FUTURE

1. "History of Witches". History.Com. Assessed May 3, 2022. https://www.history.com/topics/folklore/history-of-witches
2. "Why Do Witches Ride Brooms?". History.Com. Assessed May 3, 2022. https://www.history.com/news/why-witches-fly-on-brooms

2. ENERGY HEALING 101

1. "The Illusion of Reality: The Scientific Proof That Everything is Energy and Reality Isn't Real". http://www.esalq.usp.br/lepse/imgs/conteudo_thumb/The-Illusion-of-Reality---The-Scientific-Proof-That-Everything-is-Energy-and-Reality-Isnt-Real.pdf
2. Egnew, Thomas R. "The Meaning Of Healing: Transcending Suffering". Annals of Family Medicine. May 2005. https://www.annfammed.org/content/annalsfm/3/3/255.full.pdf
3. Yoga, Int J., *Energy Medicine*, The National Library of Medicine, January-June 2010, https://www.ncbi.nlm.nih.gov/pmc/articles/PMC2952118/
4. Trivedi, Mahendra, *Biofield Energy Signals, Energy Transmission and Neutrinos*, American Journal of Modern Physics, 2016, https://www.infona.pl/resource/bwmeta1.element.ID-b851ae2e-c93c-4b39-8416-bb6903391712
5. *5 Things Everyone Needs to Know About Energy Healing*, Growth Wellness Therapy, March 4, 2020, https://www.growthwellnesstherapy.com/our-blog/5-things-everyone-needs-to-know-about-energy-healing

6. Haley, Jolene, *Crystal Healing, History and Science Behind this Ancient Practice*, October 19, 2018, https://werewild.co/crystal-healing-history-and-science-behind-this-ancient-practice/

7. Marino, Caitlin, and The Goop Wellness Team, *Working Through Karmic Wounds*, Goop, Wellness, https://goop.com/wellness/spiri tuality/healing-karmic-wounds/

8. Allard, Syama, *5 Things to Know About Karma and Reincarnation*, Hindu American Foundation, September 4, 2020, https://www. hinduamerican.org/blog/5-things-to-know-about-karma-and-reincarnation

9. *Healing Your Mother (or Father) Wound*, Dharma Wisdom, https:// dharmawisdom.org/healing-your-mother-or-father-wound/

3. UNDERSTANDING CHAKRAS

1. Davis, Faith, *How Energy Moves Through the Chakra System*, Cosmic Cuts, January 28, 2021, https://cosmiccuts.com/blogs/healing-stones-blog/chakra-system

4. HEALING CRYSTALS 101

1. Brady, James E., and Prufer, Keith M., *Caves and Crystalmancy: Evidence for the Use of Crystals in Ancient Maya Religion*, The Journal of Anthropological Research, The University of Chicago Press, Spring 1999, https://www.jstor.org/stable/3630980

2. Carlos, Kristine D., *Crystal Healing Practices in the Western World and Beyond*, University of Central Florida, STARS, 2018, https://stars. library.ucf.edu/cgi/viewcontent.cgi?article=1283&context= honorstheses

3. Harvard Medical School, *How the Placebo Effect May Help You*, Harvard Health Publishing, May 1, 2017, https://www.health. harvard.edu/mind-and-mood/how-the-placebo-effect-may-help-you

4. Amsen, Eva, *What is a Crystal?*, Let's Talk Science, July 19, 2019, https://letstalkscience.ca/educational-resources/stem-in-context/

what-a-crystal
5. *How Do Gemstones Form?*, Gem Rock Auctions, https://www.gemrockauctions.com/learn/technical-informa tion-on-gemstones/how-do-gemstones-form
6. Yasay, Dominic, *Your Quick Guide to Crystal Shapes, Meanings, and Uses*, StoneBridge Imports, July 30, 2021 https://stonebridgeim ports.ca/a/635-your-quick-guide-to-crystal-shapes-meanings-and-uses
7. Chee, Chermaine, *How To Cleanse Crystals: 4 Ways To Cleanse Crystals*, Truly Experiences, September 27, 2021, https://trulyexperi ences.com/blog/how-to-cleanse-crystals/
8. *How To Cleanse Crystals: 9 Crucial Practices You Need To Know*, Tiny Rituals, https://tinyrituals.co/blogs/tiny-rituals/how-to-cleanse-crystals
9. *How To Program Quartz Crystals*, Sacred Gemstone, https://www.sacredgemstone.com/pages/programming-quartz-crystals
10. Abram, Christy Lynn, *How To Clean & Store Your Crystals—Plus A 6-Step Programming Technique*, Mind Body Green, June 14, 2021, https://www.mindbodygreen.com/0-14887/how-to-clear-acti vate-store-your-crystals.html

5. 34 CRYSTALS FOR BUILDING OUT YOUR CRYSTAL COLLECTION

1. *Amazonite Meaning: Healing Properties & Everyday Uses*, Tiny Rituals, https://tinyrituals.co/blogs/tiny-rituals/amazonite-meaning-stone-guide-healing-properties
2. *Amethyst Meaning: Everything You NEED To Know - Healing Properties & Everyday Uses*, Tiny Rituals, https://tinyrituals.co/blogs/tiny-rituals/amethyst-meaning-healing-properties-and-everyday-uses
3. *Angelite Meaning: Healing Properties & Everyday Uses*, Tiny Rituals, https://tinyrituals.co/blogs/tiny-rituals/angelite-meaning-heal ing-properties-everyday-uses
4. *The Meaning Of Aquamarine: Everything You Wanted To Know*, Tiny Rituals, https://tinyrituals.co/blogs/tiny-rituals/aquamarine-

meaning-stone-guide-healing-properties

5. *Obsidian Meaning: Healing Properties & Everyday Uses*, Tiny Rituals, https://tinyrituals.co/blogs/tiny-rituals/obsidian-meaning-healing-properties-everyday-uses

6. *Black Tourmaline Meaning: Healing Properties & Everyday Uses*, Tiny Rituals, https://tinyrituals.co/blogs/tiny-rituals/black-tourmaline-meaning-healing-properties-and-everyday-uses

7. *Bloodstone Meaning: Healing Properties & Everyday Uses*, Tiny Rituals, https://tinyrituals.co/blogs/tiny-rituals/bloodstone-meaning-healing-properties-everyday-uses

8. "Kyanite Meaning: Healing Properties & Everyday Uses". Tiny Rituals. https://tinyrituals.co/blogs/tiny-rituals/kyanite-meaning-healing-properties-everyday-uses

9. "Agate Meaning: Healing Properties & Everyday Uses". Tiny Rituals. https://tinyrituals.co/blogs/tiny-rituals/agate-meaning-healing-properties-everyday-uses

10. "Carnelian Meaning: Healing Properties & Everyday Uses". Tiny Rituals. https://tinyrituals.co/blogs/tiny-rituals/carnelian-meaning-healing-properties

11. "Celestite Meaning: Healing Properties & Everyday Uses". Tiny Rituals. https://tinyrituals.co/blogs/tiny-rituals/celestite-meaning-healing-properties-everyday-uses

12. "Chrysocolla Meaning: Healing Properties & Everyday Uses". Tiny Rituals. https://tinyrituals.co/blogs/tiny-rituals/chrysocolla-meaning-healing-properties-everyday-uses

13. "Citrine Meaning: Healing Properties & Everyday Uses". Tiny Rituals. https://tinyrituals.co/blogs/tiny-rituals/citrine-meaning-healing-properties

14. "Clear Quartz Meaning: Healing Properties & Uses". Tiny Rituals. https://tinyrituals.co/blogs/tiny-rituals/clear-quartz-meaning-healing-properties-uses

15. "Fluorite Meaning: Healing Properties & Everyday Uses". Tiny Rituals. https://tinyrituals.co/blogs/tiny-rituals/fluorite-meaning-healing-properties-everyday-uses

16. "Aventurine Meaning: Healing Properties & Everyday Uses". Tiny Rituals. https://tinyrituals.co/blogs/tiny-rituals/aventurine-meaning-healing-properties-everyday-uses

17. "Jade Meaning: Healing Properties & Everyday Uses. Tiny Rituals".

https://tinyrituals.co/blogs/tiny-rituals/jade-meaning-healing-properties-everyday-uses

18. "The Meaning Of Hematite: What You Need To Know - Healing Properties & More!". Tiny Rituals. https://tinyrituals.co/blogs/tiny-rituals/hematite-meaning-healing-properties-stone-guide

19. "Labradorite Meaning: All The Healing Properties & Uses You NEED To Know". Tiny Rituals. https://tinyrituals.co/blogs/tiny-rituals/labradorite-meaning-all-the-properties-you-need-to-know

20. "Lapis Lazuli Meaning: Healing Properties & Everyday Uses". Tiny Rituals. https://tinyrituals.co/blogs/tiny-rituals/lapis-lazuli-meaning-healing-properties

21. "Lepidolite Meaning: Healing Properties & Everyday Use". Tiny Rituals. https://tinyrituals.co/blogs/tiny-rituals/lepidolite-meaning-healing-properties-everyday-use

22. "Malachite Meaning: Healing Properties & Everyday Uses". Tiny Rituals. https://tinyrituals.co/blogs/tiny-rituals/malachite-meaning-healing-properties

23. "Moonstone Meaning: Healing Properties & Everyday Uses". Tiny Rituals. https://tinyrituals.co/blogs/tiny-rituals/moonstone-meaning-healing-properties-everyday-uses

24. "Peridot Meaning: Healing Properties & Everyday Uses". Tiny Rituals. https://tinyrituals.co/blogs/tiny-rituals/peridot-meaning-stone-guide-healing-properties

25. "Pyrite Meaning: Healing Properties & Everyday Uses". Tiny Rituals. https://tinyrituals.co/blogs/tiny-rituals/pyrite-meaning-healing-properties-everyday-uses

26. "Garnet Meaning: Healing Properties & Everyday Uses". Tiny Rituals. https://tinyrituals.co/blogs/tiny-rituals/garnet-meaning-healing-properties

27. "Red Jasper Meaning: Healing Properties & Everyday Uses". Tiny Rituals. https://tinyrituals.co/blogs/tiny-rituals/red-jasper-meaning-healing-properties-and-everyday-uses

28. "Rhodonite Meaning: Healing Properties & Everyday Uses". Tiny Rituals. https://tinyrituals.co/blogs/tiny-rituals/rhodonite-meaning-healing-properties-everyday-uses

29. "Rose Quartz Meaning: Healing Properties And Everyday Uses". Tiny Rituals. https://tinyrituals.co/blogs/tiny-rituals/rose-quartz-

meaning-healing-properties-and-everyday-uses
30. "Selenite Meaning: Healing Properties & Everyday Uses". Tiny Rituals. https://tinyrituals.co/blogs/tiny-rituals/selenite-meaning-healing-properties-everyday-uses
31. "Smoky Quartz Meaning: Healing Properties & Everyday Uses". Tiny Rituals. https://tinyrituals.co/blogs/tiny-rituals/smoky-quartz-meaning-healing-properties-everyday-uses
32. "The Meaning Of Sodalite: The Ultimate Guide". Tiny Rituals. https://tinyrituals.co/blogs/tiny-rituals/sodalite-meaning-stone-guide-healing-properties
33. "Tigers Eye Meaning: Secrets & Healing Properties Revealed". Tiny Rituals. https://tinyrituals.co/blogs/tiny-rituals/tiger-eye-meaning-and-uses
34. "Turquoise Meaning: Physical, Emotional, & Spiritual Healing Properties". Tiny Rituals. https://tinyrituals.co/blogs/tiny-rituals/turquoise-howlite-meaning-healing-properties-and-everyday-uses

7. HARNESSING THE POWER OF YOUR CRYSTALS

1. Scialla, Janelle, *A Brief History of Crystals and Healing*, Crystal Age, https://www.crystalage.com/crystal_information/crystal_history/
2. Askinosie, Heather, 8 Ways To Use Crystals In Your Everyday Routine, Mind Body Green, January 31, 2020, https://www.mindbodygreen.com/0-23590/8-lesserknown-ways-to-use-crystals-in-your-everyday-routine.html
3. Askinosie, Heather, *A Room-by-Room Guide to Using Crystals for the Home*, Energy Muse, January 18, 2019, https://www.energymuse.com/blog/using-crystals-for-the-home-and-interior-design

8. 5 EASY STEPS TO PERFORM A
CRYSTAL HEALING SPELL

1. Khan, Nina, *11 Easy One-Minute Crystal Rituals That Will Help You Attract All The Good Vibes*, Bustle, December 4, 2018, https://www.bustle.com/p/11-easy-one-minute-crystal-rituals-to-try-even-if-youre-a-crystal-newbie-13242074

2. Team Elle, *Healing Crystals - What Are They And How Should You Use Them?*, Elle Magazine, July 5, 2021, https://www.elle.com/uk/life-and-culture/culture/articles/a31572/what-are-healing-crystals-how-to-use-them/

Printed in Great Britain
by Amazon

36013153R00155